~ Chad's book brings you to the angst of g(
reader understand the issues a child experi
you've never experienced gender confusion
world as a child, teenager, and adult. And he doesn't disappoint. ~
~ Kimberly Morin

~ Few among us don't know the temptation and allure of wanting a quick medical fix for our problems, whether surgery or medication. In his heartbreaking memoir, Chad Felix Greene shows us that those options don't fix us, they often break us, and being true to yourself is far more about acceptance than change. '~
~ Libby Emmons

~ Touching, wry, raw and wise, Chad Felix Greene's memoir is a must-read and an enormous contribution to the public conversation on gender identity. ~
~ Abigail Shrier

~ Gender dysphoria is obviously a complex topic with a lot of layers. In this book, Chad Felix Greene does an excellent job of taking readers through his story and how life experiences can play a critical role in developing one's identity. Aside from providing an interesting account of his life, Chad also leaves the reader with several relevant lessons to consider in determining how they think about Gender Dysphoria and potential responses to it.

    I would highly recommend this book to anyone that wants to better understand how someone with gender dysphoria may feel, how those feelings can be affected by the society around them, and what are the potential implications for the various solutions that are now considered the norm. ~
~ AG Hamilton

Surviving Gender

Chad Felix Greene

Surviving Gender

My Journey Through Gender Dysphoria

Copyright © Chad Felix Greene 2022
Surviving Gender
All rights Reserved
ISBN: 9798839386082
Imprint: Independently published
www. chadfelixgreene. com
First Edition
Printing 2022
Printed in the United State of America

The stories within contain personal details and retelling of events. No names were used and in some cases, identity information has been changed to protect the individual from recognition. Many of the individuals referenced are alive and were not involved in the creation of this book. All details are accurate to the best of my knowledge.

The author and publisher do not assume and hereby disclaim any liability to any party for any loss, damage, or disruption caused by errors or omissions, whether such errors or omissions result from negligence, accident, or any other cause.

No part of this book may be reproduced, scanned, or distributed in any printed or electronic form without permission. Please do not participate in or encourage piracy of copyrighted materials in violation of the author's rights.

My husband Jacob who has patiently walked with me every step of the way on this journey.

Ryan T. Anderson, who took a chance and published my personal story and gave me the courage to speak out on the issue of gender identity in children.

Abigail Shrier, who courageously revealed to the world what was happening to young women and inspired me to speak out on behalf of young men.

WARNING: This book contains autobiographical stories involving graphic details of the author's experience with psychological, physical and sexual abuse as a child and a minor.

Contents

	Introduction	i
Chapter One	My First Memory	1
Chapter Two	My Favorite Color	13
Chapter Three	My Grandmother's Rings	27
Chapter Four	Uncle Vince	37
Chapter Five	Losing My Faith	49
Chapter Six	Twink	63
Chapter Seven	Could I Really Be a Girl?	81
Chapter Eight	Life	113
Chapter Nine	More Than Surviving	137
	Epilogue	157
	Published Articles	169

If 'Transphobia' Exists, it is Entirely The LGBT Movement's Doing	169
Gender Identity: Embracing My Masculinity	176
To #ProtectTransKids We Must Address Child Exploitation and Sexual Abuse	182
Transgender Suicides: What to Do About Them	188
I Was an Eight-Year-Old Drag Queen	193
Why LGBT Activists Can't See What's Wrong With A 9-Year-Old Drag Queen	199
Here's Why I Choose Life Instead Of Ending It Like My Dad Did	202
The Atlantic's Article Should Foster A Consensus That Transgenderism Is Adults-Only	207
My Rape Doesn't Justify Punishing People Without Due Process	212
Even Though I Feel Non-Binary, Identifying As My Biological Sex Makes Sense. Here's Why	216
How Ryan Anderson's Banned Book, 'When Harry Became Sally,' Helped Me With Gender Dysphoria	221

Appendix	227
Notes	237

Introduction

In 2015, guidelines were issued by The American Psychological Association's (APA) Task Force on Guidelines for Psychological Practice with Transgender and Gender Nonconforming People.

According to the guidelines, "Transgender and gender nonconforming people are those who have a gender identity that is not fully aligned with their sex assigned at birth." The foundation of this official medical perspective is based on an ideological belief that biological sex, the objective recognition of primary and secondary sexual characteristics, is "assigned" by doctors at birth.

"Psychologists understand that gender is a nonbinary construct that allows for a range of gender identities and that a person's gender identity may not align with sex assigned at birth." Gender Identity is defined as, "a person's deeply felt, inherent sense of being a girl, woman, or female; a boy, a man, or male; a blend of male or female; or an alternative gender." Gender, within this worldview, is an identity that can only be defined by the individual based on their "deeply felt" perceptions of what a boy or a girl must feel like.

The guideline argues, "For TGNC [Transgender and Gender Non-Conforming People] people, gender identity differs from sex assigned at birth to varying degrees and may be experienced and expressed outside of the gender binary."[1]

In the years since, advocacy has grown louder from both sides of the argument, over whether a child should be transitioned, socially, or through medical intervention. Conflicting statistics, activist researchers, politics, rhetoric, and heightened emotions have largely made this discussion impossible.

There have been books and other media by conservative authors diving into the studies, the politics, and the medical justification for transition, including Ryan T. Anderson's 2018 book, *When Harry Became Sally*, Abigail Shrier's 2021 book, *Irreversible Damage: The Transgender Craze Seducing Our Daughters*, and Matt Walsh's 2022 documentary, *What is a Woman?*

I recommend all these titles and support the perspectives they provide. Each is a compassionate and objective look into the issue, with analysis, research, and personal stories. I decided that perhaps adding my own experience might benefit this larger discussion.

I have been "out" as a transgender person since around 2014 or 2015. Prior to that, I didn't really identify with the label because I never transitioned. By this time in my own journey, I had largely found peace with my sense of gender and generally assumed it was all part of being gay.

But as the debate began to heat up and transgender arguments moved further away from individual freedom and towards collective coercion, I felt it was important to speak out. I had always supported transgender individuals in their efforts to live as the other sex and advocated for their right to do so legally and without harassment. Truthfully, this wasn't a particularly controversial stance to hold within the conservative movement.

It was only when activists began insisting that identity alone was sufficient for public and legal recognition, complete with full access to all sex-segregated spaces, that conservatives began to object. It was certainly one thing for a fully transitioned transwoman to enter a woman's restroom without anyone noticing, and quite another for an obvious male to do so with the intention of abusing new discrimination laws and policies for the purpose of spying on or targeting women and girls.[2,3]

Gender identity without transition contrasted with the growing demand that children as young as two were capable of understanding their gender and parents had a moral responsibility to provide them "life-saving healthcare," and begin preparing them for transition. This involved using medical intervention to "pause" puberty.

For many, this was a line crossed, myself included, and conservatives began to speak out against the practice as more and more medical authorities and organizations adopted progressive ideological stances on gender, biological sex and the recommended medical treatment of children with gender dysphoria.

So, I began to share my own experiences with gender dysphoria and how I seemingly grew out of it on my own. In 2017, I published my first professional piece titled, *Transgender Suicides: What to Do About Them*, on *Public Discourse*, where I argued, "In order to achieve a healthy and mentally stable state, a trans person must have their gender and sex as closely aligned as possible. Why, though, does this require the physical sex to change in order to align to the perceived gender? Why shouldn't the perceived gender be what changes?"[4]

That had been my own experience and in my extensive discussions with transgender activists, I had only received hostility in return for asking it. Despite my clear experience with gender dysphoria as a child, activists dismissed my perspective claiming I wasn't *really* trans.

However, this only strengthened my argument that if there was no way to know who was really trans and who was not, how could doctors possibly justify placing a child on a permanent path to medical transition? In May of 2022, the American Academy of Pediatrics (AAP), released a study titled, *Gender Identity 5 Years*

After Social Transition, reporting that most children who transition early, persist in their gender identity.

As reported by the *New York Times*, "Young children who transition to a new gender with social changes — taking on new names, pronouns, haircuts and clothing — are likely to continue identifying as that gender five years later," the report continued, "The data come from the Trans Youth Project, a well-known effort following 317 children across the United States and Canada who underwent a so-called social transition between ages of 3 and 12. Participants transitioned, on average, at age 6.5."

In the study, which followed 317 transgender youth, at a median age of eight years at the start of the study, reported 2.5 percent reverted to their original gender. Most of the children, 94 percent, persisted in their new gender by the end of the study. Curiously, 7.3 percent of the children "retransitioned" at least once during the time period, indicting a shift from identifying as the opposite sex, then the original sex and back to the opposite sex again.

The study noted, "Later cisgender identities were more common amongst youth whose initial social transition occurred before age 6 years; the retransition often occurred before age 10."[5]

The *Times*, however, also notes that 60 percent of the children had begun taking puberty blockers by the end of the study. Amy Tishelman, a clinical psychologist at Boston College and lead author of the World Professional Association of Transgender Health's standards of care chapter on children, argued, "Some people may say that kids get on this trajectory of development, and they can't get off and that the medical interventions may be irreversible and they may come to regret it," she said. "Other people will say kids know their gender, and when they're supported in their gender, they're happy."

The *Times* concluded, arguing, "In our work we don't just want to know what category they fit in today vs. tomorrow," Dr. Olson said. "I think of all these kids as gender diverse in different ways," she added, "and we want to understand how to help their lives be better."[6]

A 2018 study of the research conducted in Italy titled, *Attachment Patterns and Complex Trauma in a Sample of Adults Diagnosed with Gender Dysphoria*, published in the journal, *Front.Psychol.*, provides a contradictory view, in which researchers argued, "Many children who experience GD do not continue to experience it after puberty. Studies have found the percentage of persistence into adolescence and adulthood to vary from 2 to 20%." This indicates that upwards of 80 percent of children allowed to continue on into puberty without medical intervention do *not* continue identifying as or wishing to be the opposite sex.[7]

In 1994, a breakthrough study titled, *Transsexualism, Dissociation, and Child Abuse*, published in the *Journal of Psychology & Human Sexuality* interviewed 45 male to female transgender individuals and reported, "Sixty percent reported one or more types of severe child abuse. In the course of discussing other issues, participants also reported having experienced many of the commonly cited initial and long-term effects of child abuse, including fear, anxiety and depression, eating disorders, substance abuse, excessive aggression, and suicide ideation and attempts."

The study author argued, "I have speculated, as have some of the participants themselves, that, in some cases, transsexualism may be an adaptive extreme dissociative swival response to severe child abuse."[8] Complex trauma is defined by the above-mentioned Italian study as "a set of experiences of cumulative, chronic and prolonged traumatic events, most often of an interpersonal nature, involving primary caregivers and frequently arising in early childhood or adolescence."

The study confirmed from the collected research, "Regarding early traumas, 56% experienced four or more traumatic forms. Further, gender dysphoric adults showed significantly higher levels of attachment disorganization and polyvictimisation, relative to controls." Continued, "Comparisons of subgroups, defined by natal gender, showed that trans women, compared to control males, had more involving and physically and psychologically abusive fathers, and were more often separated from their mothers; trans men, relative to female controls, had more involving mothers and were more frequently separated from and neglected by their fathers."

Further examination of complex trauma concluded, "Maltreatment experiences may include: severe neglect; exposure to domestic violence; intensive, painful medical conditions; and physical and sexual abuse. Often, children suffering from complex trauma face a combination of these experiences."

"The relationship between relational trauma and GD has often been described as univocal. Many authors have speculated about the influence of trauma, abuse, dysfunctional parental conduct (such as a mother's extreme closeness with her child), parental dynamics or pathology (such as maternal depression or the absence of a father) and parents' atypical psychosexual development (such as their confusion about their own feelings of masculinity and femininity) on children. It has been thought that such environmental patterns might limit children's opportunities to identify with the same-sex parent and to experience cross-gender reinforcement patterns."

In another reviewed study, "The authors also found an impressively high frequency of traumatic experiences within the first 10 years of life." Around 70 percent of various cohorts of individuals indicated a high level of "insecure attachment" to their parents. A 2017 study found 66 percent of the study cohort had "traumatic childhood experiences relating to the loss of an attachment figure or physical or sexual abuse." One study showed that "patients in gender clinics were more likely than psychiatric patients to report parental death during adolescence and early adulthood."

The conclusion of the study indicated gaps in the available literature and sought to conduct its own research. Utilizing complex psychological evaluation testing with 95 transgender participants, it found 65 percent had experienced multiple severe early childhood physical and/or sexual trauma. In comparison 7 percent of the control group of 123 gender typical individuals reported the same results. *[See Appendix, Figure 1]*

When compared with a similar clinical sample of individuals suffering from dissociative and personality disorders, there was no difference in evaluated repeated, severe trauma in early childhood. *[See Appendix, Figure 2]* "The environment provided by maltreating parents usually induces children to develop dissociative and avoidant strategies to cope with extreme emotions and this prevents them from processing and normatively integrating memories and experiences."

This comparison remained consistent between transmen and transwomen within all control groups. The study specifically compared gender typical males to gender dysphoric males, and the same for females, "Trans women, compared to control males: (1) were more neglected by both parents; (2) had more involving, rejecting and physically and psychologically abusive fathers; and (3) suffered more frequently from an early loss of the father. On the other hand, trans men, compared to female controls: (1) were more often victims of intensive rejection, neglect and early separation from fathers; (2) had more psychologically abusive mothers; and (3) prematurely experienced more losses of close relatives and friends."

What stood out to researchers in the comparisons was "For the trans women, idealization of mothers could be interpreted as idealization of the feminine figure or feminine aspects they felt were their own."[9-23,24-40, 7,41-43]

I decided to share my own story because I fall into that 2.5 percent category of kids who initially reported an alternative gender only to later embrace their biological sex, and I never experienced social or medical transition. I also fall into the wide array of studies proposing a strong link between gender dysphoria and early childhood psychological, physical and sexual abuse.

While many activists insist this small percentage of cases does not indicate a trend or justification for making decisions about all medical and social interventions for children, I have consistently argued it does. Partially due to the near complete reversal of study outcomes after more aggressive medical intervention and socialization became the medical norm, and partially because I believe those voices have to be heard.

In writing this story, I share some of my deepest and most profoundly vulnerable thoughts and experiences in the hopes that those engaged in debate over this controversy will see both sides of the argument and rethink assumptions. I lived with gender dysphoria as a child, I suffered through confusion, insecurity, and doubt as an adult, and I came out the other side happy and content in my natural body. That experience, I believe, deserves consideration.

I can't speak for the lives of others who have gone through similar struggles, and I don't pretend to be an expert on what is correct or incorrect in determining medical treatment, but I do know what it's like to feel betrayed by your body and lost in your sense of gender. All I can offer is my own journey and hope that it provides a different perspective in understanding what gender means to all of us

ONE

My First Memory

My first memory, the first moment of self-awareness I can bring to the surface with emotion and vivid clarity, is me in bed staring up at the popcorn ceiling in my bedroom at seven years old and pleading with God to let me wake up as a girl. I can still feel the hopelessness wrapped inside faithful words as tears blurred my vision and I tried to keep my voice as low as possible, but just loud enough for God to hear. Every night I would repeat the same tearful plea and every morning I would wake up sad. For most of my life I just thought I was a broken boy, a boy that had to make it long enough to get from one safe place to the next.

In a world nearly vibrating with positive messaging to "be yourself" and not give into peer pressure, I felt trapped in a body that mocked such a notion. When it slipped out, like in the 3rd grade when I glanced over at a girl I admired because she was nice to me and she was popular and I mimicked her graceful swan-like raising of her hand in class, it instantaneously brought torment. Being myself was dangerous. The only exception was when I was alone with my grandmother who seemed to appreciate my femininity, filtered through an idealistic belief in how a polite and mature young man should behave, where I could relax my body, forget my maleness and simply be.

I don't remember my life before the age of seven, but I have a lot of photos my grandmother kept safe for me in a shoebox of that time. When I shuffle through them, I see so many familiar settings, my grandmother's kitchen, the living room in our trailer where my dad hung his collection of baseball caps, but I don't remember me. I see a child that I recognize, but I don't feel a connection, just a vague sense that I must have existed because there I am. The boy I see, however, tells me a story. In each scene, usually a holiday or my birthday or some special event my grandmother felt needed to be preserved, I see a boy not quite sure of himself, but full of personality.

That child was clearly vocal and expressive in who he wanted to be and as it turns out, when I later came out as gay, no one was surprised. My body movements, frozen in a moment, reflect excitement, fluidity, and a pronounced lack of self-awareness. My arms extended, my head tilted to one side, my legs bent in a pose, and my face lit up with joy, performing and dancing. When I posed for a picture, I posed like an adult version of me traveled back in time making sure to leave sufficient evidence of my inherent fabulousness. I stood out.

I always stood out. In school plays where there was a line of stiff-armed kids smiling straight ahead into the audience I am routinely found to be smiling at the camera, my waist bent, my arms posed to my sides or waving and my legs in mid-dance. I am told that when I was performing, usually for my grandmother, that I was a radiant child. I seemed to only exist in sheer exuberance or deep inner seclusion, hiding from the world. I didn't get along with the other kids, typically shadowing adults around babbling away, and I didn't have any friends.

I was also very clear and very adamant that if the option were available, I wanted to be a girl. I apparently spoke of nothing else. My grandmother told me of how I would chatter on and on about how much nicer it would be if I could just be a girl. I could play with the toys I wanted, I could wear pink clothes, I could sing and dance as much as I wanted, and I could have long hair. I could be like her, I would insist. She thought it was a phase, something I would grow out of once my dad met a nice woman and I had a mother. My parents divorced when I was two and my mother took my sister with her when she left.

My grandmother reasoned that my young brain decided my mom preferred girls and didn't like boys and if I had been a girl, she would have taken me with her too. I even believed that I was the reason she left, and thought perhaps had I been a girl, she wouldn't have.

The separation was very sudden, I woke up to my mom making me breakfast to her not coming home that evening after fighting with my dad and then not seeing her again until I was seven. I was apparently also deeply resentful of my little sister, once pushing her car seat off the couch with it landing upside down and her still in it.

So rather than address my femininity and vocal desire to be a girl, she played along believing it would pass on its own once I found confidence in my place in the family again. In other ways she enjoyed my sweet feminine nature, avoiding the more common issues boys of that age go through. It seems I was very well spoken and intellectually curious and she could take me to her bridge group, and I'd watch and play and chat along with her friends. I preferred being around women and openly refused to be left alone with men.

The only exception seemed to be my grandfather, who I was extremely close to and would spend hours in the evenings watching TV or examining his coin collection when my dad worked his second job and my grandmother cooked or cleaned up after dinner. My grandfather was a generally unpleasant man very few people got along with. He and my grandmother met as teenagers, quickly got married after he left the navy and after two kids and five decades together had grown to merely tolerate each other's presence. But with me they found a common joy and purpose and I am told my grandfather cried in front of the family when he held me at my birth.

Upon reaching an age where my memories begin to trickle in, I recall being happy with my grandparents, miserable and afraid at school, fighting with my dad and feeling a constant pressure to change everything about myself to make everyone else happy. These moments of emotion still bubble up through me when I conjure them, and I can still feel the sensation of disappointment, fear and relief depending on where I was allowed to be at any given moment. It is remarkable how my memory just begins with such force and how the tangible ripples of those memories still impact me even as I write this.

So much of my memory focuses on my internal sense of simply not being correct in whatever setting I found myself in. Sitting in class and watching the other students, trying to study their behavior and decode what it was they were thinking and how it was so easy for them to enjoy each other's company. I would watch the girls with longing, unconsciously mimicking their movements, vocal patterns, and facial expressions as they giggled amongst each other. In comparison the boys always seemed to be aware of me, laughing and mocking.

It was the feeling that my body was an obstacle that I remember the most. I never used the bathroom at school, if I could help it, but I knew that boys engaged differently together than girls did in these private spaces. I chose to avoid them entirely fearing the isolation and vulnerability. Although I never remember viewing my privates in any specific way or even being aware of the difference between myself and girls, I do remember assuming I must have been different myself in some way.

A game I was accidentally very good at involved the jungle gym which was an assortment of different metal bars at differing heights for kids to easily hurt themselves on. I still have a scar on my lower lip where I slipped on a dewy bar one morning and landed on my chin, pushing my tooth through. The game was a challenge where you sat on the bar next to a competitor, gripped the bar on either side and then flung yourself backwards catching the bar with your knees, spinning forward and back up onto the bar and doing it again. The winner was the one who could do the most flips. For an added challenge you could straddle the bar, locking your knee around it as you fell backwards with your other leg straight out, returning to position with the bar between your legs.

This part is what earned me a great deal of mockery from the boys who watched us play, which exclusively involved girls and myself, because straddling the bar and landing on it with each rotation got a "*ooooh!!*" from them believing it must hurt. I prided myself on it not hurting which brought them to the conclusion I had nothing between my legs. Strangely this was comforting to me because although I knew I did have something between my legs, I had no Earthly idea what other kids looked like naked, so I came to believe mine were somehow either like the girls who also didn't get hurt in the game, or something else entirely.

This made me more like the girls than the boys and in that one public exercise of skill, I felt triumphant in finding my place among my peers, even within the mixture of impressed jeering and mockery from the boys. It occurred to me then that I obviously was not like the other boys because they all seemed to be in agreement that the bar game was only for girls, and they were physically incapable of playing. Flipping around on a bar, it seems, was my first validation that I was always going to be different from the boys I was forced by adults to be segregated with.

Sadly, one of the boys got the idea to put a rock on the ground behind me one day as a prank and when I flung myself backwards, I bashed the back of my head into the rock, forcing the teachers to put an end to the game forever. I still snuck over to the playground by myself in the evenings, as it was within walking distance of my home, and would recapture the thrill of falling backwards with complete reckless abandon, seeing the world as a blur of colors and the wind zipping around my hair as it played in my face.

For a time, my grandmother let my hair grow out because absolutely everyone thought it was the most beautiful thing they'd ever seen. I had wavy and curly light reddish blonde hair and at one point it was to my shoulders wet. Thanks to Billie Ray Cyrus, it was shaped into a mullet and therefore deemed socially acceptable. I even had racer stripes cut into the side above my ears for an extra layer of coolness. It was my father's idea.

I profoundly loved my hair. I distinctly remember staring in the mirror and shaking it, flipping it, and laughing as it fell all around my face wet, only to curl up and look more like a boyish bob as it dried. My grandmother loved to brush it out with me after a bath and we would talk about so many things. She even highlighted my hair with the blonde she used on her own.

My hair felt like me. I was the most myself with my hair. My dad, however, was only tolerant of it because it got women to approach us to tell us how cute I was and sometimes got him dates. He hated that I was feminine though, constantly trying to shame or punish it out of me. I remember constantly hiding from him believing I was something he absolutely despised. Although it was just him and me in our small trailer, I spent most of my time with my grandmother while he worked. He had me when he was in his early 20s and was still building his own life while shamefully becoming a quite sudden single father. He saw my lack of boyishness as a failure on his part.

This meant that every single day of my childhood memory with him was a battle of hiding myself to avoid his anger, disappointment and often, his tears. He once walked in on me in the bathroom brushing my hair and singing to myself and I guess the image was too much for him and I found him angrily crying in the dark in his bedroom.

To me this felt like what I imagined hell to be. I went to sleep every night crying and praying to wake up as a girl and I woke up every morning disappointed, angry, and deeply hopeless. I believed my dad might not love me as much if I was a girl, but I knew I could never be the kind of boy he wanted me to be.

That type of boy was, of course, what all other boys seemed to be like. The kind I knew I was very different from after the bar flip game. Upon my revelation, I even excitedly reported to him that maybe I wasn't a boy at all, hoping it would inspire new options in his head. It only angered him, and he became embarrassed that I was engaging in the activity at all and giving the other boys ammunition against me.

I couldn't seem to effectively express the inherent struggles I had fitting in. When I would bring up the topic of being a girl and if it would be easier on all of us, he shut it down immediately, frequently violently. I felt trapped and frustrated. It seemed like the perfect solution to the problem, and I already wasn't a regular boy to begin with. My arguments were not persuasive.

Despite my failures at convincing him of my plan, which I assumed was a requirement to begin whatever it was that would successfully turn me into a girl, I kept exploring the secret lives of girls anyway. I would spend my reading time at school tucked away in a corner, hiding books meant for girls inside larger textbooks, hoping to find the answer.

On one occasion while at one of his girlfriend's houses, I decided to go to the source directly. She had a daughter who was twelve or thirteen and she would babysit me when they went out on dates. One evening he came home to find us in her bedroom playing with Barbie dolls. I remember combing through the doll's hair contently when suddenly my father burst into the room shouting angrily, grabbing me by the arm and jerking me upwards dislocating my shoulder.

The pain was so intense, and I felt this overwhelming sense of terror as his girlfriend and her daughter frantically rushed around us, everyone shouting at once. I must have passed out as my next memory was in bed with a sore shoulder and my father staring at me, obviously upset, with obvious evidence of recent tears, and me telling him I was sorry for making him mad. I was always trying to make him feel better, trying to make him happier and I only ever seemed to hurt him more.

For me, I thought the thing that pushed him over the edge was that the doll was naked. I hadn't decided on her outfit yet and being obsessed with long, flowing hair, I wanted to use my limited time to indulge that enjoyment. During the altercation, I repeatedly tried to convince him that I wasn't doing anything sinful or shameful. I wasn't playing with the nude doll for inappropriate reasons. I didn't fully understand where his anger was coming from, and he was extremely poor at articulating his feelings.

A breaking point for him came when I was put on a baseball team and my complete lack of athletic ability, or interest, was on full display. I was always put in right field because it was the furthest position away from anything meaningful happening on the field. My job was to pay attention in case a ball flew to my corner and then try to catch it.

Instead, I tended to get bored watching the distant activity and mumbled shouting. Out in the field, far away from everyone else, I would become fixated on a butterfly or a nearby flower and frequently had to be aggressively shouted at to snap me out of my daydream. Once the annoyance from my coaches turned into genuine panic because a ball was in the air, on its way to smack me directly in the head and I wasn't paying attention.

I was probably spinning around, talking to myself or singing, completely obvious to my surroundings the day my dad finally lost his patience. I was a profound embarrassment to him in front of his friends who were too busy proudly cheering on their own sons. I would hear my name echoing towards me and finally look up to see my dad angrily flailing his arms and demanding I play the game correctly.

The line crossed, however, was one day when a coach from another team approached my dad to talk about the teams and pointed at me, turned around with only my hair flowing in the wind and asked who the little girl was. My dad punched the man in the face, and I once again found myself being jerked out of blissful, solitary fantasy by an angry raving father and going home.

My hair was gone that night. I still remember looking in the mirror at myself, my hair taken from me, my only sense of personal authenticity and joy stolen, and softly crying. I cried softly as to not allow my dad to hear me, knowing it would anger him again. I remember just looking at myself, feeling betrayed, beaten up and so deeply sad, trying not to let a single sob escape my lips.

My last moment of unselfconscious freedom came earlier that day when I was in the dugout waiting for my turn to go to bat and bending forward with my hair in my helmet and then pulling it off and flipping my hair backwards. I did it over and over again completely unaware of the group of boys staring at me like I was a crazy person.

I remember one boy asking the coach what in the world I was doing to which he awkwardly remarked I was probably just trying to cool off. No, in truth I was loving flipping my hair back and forth and feeling it blow around in the wind and over my face. The motion was an intoxicating mixture of dizziness, disorientation and feeling like I was floating away. It was the one part of myself that felt unregulated and free. It didn't make me a girl, but it let me not be a boy just long enough to stop thinking about it.

My grandmother was furious with my dad and his growing irrational reactions to my behavior. She would tell me later on that she tried to explain that not all boys are big, manly, gruff brutes like him, but he was determined to make sure I wouldn't turn out queer. Everything pointed to me being a sissy and he could think of absolutely nothing more embarrassing or more evident of his failure as a father. It seemed nothing else I accomplished in my life ever quite made up for that sense of loss in his mind.

I was a creative child, but a lonely one. I spent most of my time outside, alone on the riverbank behind my house, telling myself stories. I built an entire world down there, the foundation made by my grandfather who cleared a nice, safe path to the water's edge. I crafted tiny villages and twirled around in blissful abandon telling stories of the adventures happening there. No one could see or hear me, and I was perfectly content.

It was also a place where I could experiment with being girly, even fashioning long wigs out of grass and flowers as well as skirts. I would prance back and forth pretending to be a fairy or sit in the water and act out scenes from *The Little Mermaid*, my favorite movie. Hidden by thick brush along a ten-foot-high dirt wall, I could be absolutely anything. I often sat for hours staring out at the river in a trance, fantasizing that a beautiful mermaid would appear and turn me into one and take me with her.

In my room at night, I would cautiously and quietly continue my stories, wishes and prayers, and flit around my room, pausing every so often for signs that my father was nearby. I had several sports games and toys, courtesy of him, and they were always at the ready if my door were to suddenly open. Even there I was not safe.

At one point I became fascinated with gymnastics. I think one of my friends at school showed off her flipping skills and I instantly felt inspired. One particular skill the girls loved to show off was their ability to slide into a perfect split with ease. This, above all, was my goal. But I was tall for my age, with long limbs that did not seem willing to flex in the direction I wanted them to. I practiced every night in my room and despite all my efforts, I could never get closer than half-way to the floor.

One evening, to my horror, as I was at the breaking point of my flexibility, my dad unexpectedly opened my door and caught me. For a moment he stared in disbelief that quickly grew into anger and he shouted, demanding to know what I was doing. I had no answer, no easily available excuse, no logical reason for my behavior.

I sort of crumbled over into a sitting position and stared back, helpless, terrified. After he exhausted his rage trying desperately to beat his own fears out of me, he stared once more at my sobbing, broken body with disgust and shut my door. I never achieved my goal of doing the splits.

TWO

My Favorite Color

My favorite colors were pink and yellow. From before I can remember, all my art included these two colors as the primary theme. Somehow the two in combination felt like freedom to me. I can still remember gazing down as the crayon glided across the paper and seeing these precious colors radiate back to me and feeling peaceful and happy. I reasoned that the yellow reasonably concealed the fact that pink was involved and wouldn't draw negative attention. Pink was the true star.

It was a strange time to be a boy in the late 80's and early 90's. Neon colors were everywhere, and that included the brightest of hot pinks, which were common in clothing for boys. I often felt a moment of hope when my classmates flooded into class and some of the boys were wearing items with hot pink on them. My eyes would light up and I would lock onto one of them, carefully studying his movements, how the other boys interacted with him and cross referencing this new information with everything I knew about him. The boys mocked me for coloring in pink or saying pink was my favorite color, but they seemed perfectly comfortable wearing pink themselves.

Ironically, I was not permitted to wear anything with the forbidden color on it. Even when I casually mentioned at the store that so-and-so at school wore this exact same shirt, my dad ignored me. But in a way, the option even being available was enough to bring me hope. Maybe one day I could wear pink too and no one would care.

At some point I must have gotten a small pin of hot pink sunglasses from a gumball machine, as I have a few photos of myself wearing it when I was five or six. I loved that pin because it was one of the few pink things I was allowed to own. It was kept safely at my grandmother's house in a small wooden box my grandfather gave me to hold my treasures. That box sits on my bookshelf with all of those treasures still inside.

Alongside it were rhinestones and sequins I found on the floor under clothing racks while shopping with my grandmother, rings I secretly won in gumball machines and any other sparkling jewel I could find. My pin was always there, waiting for me to share in its bright and worry-free joy. As soon as I came home from school I would run upstairs, take my treasure box from my grandfather's display cabinet, and put on my pin. It was as if that small plastic object acted as an amulet, allowing me to transform into my true self without anyone else seeing.

Everything in my life was a secret. From how long I let myself look at the women on the covers of magazines on my grandmother's coffee table, to the precise amount of time I knew I could play with my hair before my father became suspicious. I knew which songs I could sing in front of people, and which had to be hidden away in a closet or reserved for my townspeople by the river. Every movement was carefully measured against the reactions from others and the watchful eye of my father.

I was always looking for evidence to support my argument that my interests were acceptable. Always searching for some loophole to the rules. If I saw a boy on TV dancing or passed a man in pink at the mall or noticed even the slightest indication of femininity in any man I encountered, on TV, in cartoons or in magazines, I would eagerly point them out to my father. I hoped with enough reasoning and evidence, my father would realize nothing was wrong me and perhaps, simply leave me alone.

By sheer accident, one evening at the mall with my grandparents, I found myself walking through the magazine isle blissfully unaware of my surroundings when I stumbled upon a cover that shocked my senses. I was about 10 and the magazine was for extreme bodybuilders. The cover featured an impossibly muscular, almost entirely nude man posing with an even more impossibly muscular, and equally as exposed, woman. The sight was absolutely confounding to me.

To add to the assault on my senses was the fact that both were wearing the tiniest underwear I'd ever seen, and they were both hot pink. How could a man so powerfully representative of the highest achievement of masculinity be wearing pink, and to my eyes, women's underwear? Furthermore, I had never seen a muscular woman before, certainly not to the proportions displayed there. Were these special kinds of people? Were they superheroes?

My 10-year-old brain, excited by the new images and their influence on my growing hormones, was simply overwhelmed with possibility. If a man could dress like a girl and a girl could look like a man and it was on a magazine cover for all to see, was there an entire world out there I was missing? I had to know more. I knew, however, that my grandmother would probably not be as eager to indulge my curiosity since both the man and the woman were essentially naked. I also assumed there was a risk my dad would notice the pink underwear the man was wearing and equally disapprove.

Despite my misgivings, I decided to chance it anyway as I had to know more about what I was witnessing. As casually as a 10-year-old can, I took the magazine, rolled it up and strolled over to my grandmother who was busy shopping and didn't seem to notice. When we got to the checkout, I slyly slipped the magazine face-down, on the moving belt and held my breath as I watched it slink slowly to the cashier.

My grandmother, not so easily fooled, quickly noticed my scheme, and grabbed the magazine. She flipped it over, scanned the cover, narrowed her eyes, looked down at me and asked what exactly I thought I was buying. I quickly blurted out something about my dad wanting me to start exercising and it was an exercise magazine after all. Her eyes narrowed further and her decision clear, she put it on top of the magazine rack and randomly selected a less extreme exercise magazine that was conveniently nearby as a suitable replacement.

"I don't think your father would want you seeing such inappropriate images of women like that," she reasoned, causing me a moment of relief realizing she noticed the mostly naked woman and not the mostly naked man. I assured her, honestly, that I had absolutely no nefarious motivation in my choice regarding the woman. I was a good Christian boy, after all, and I respected women. She approved of my defense, and tossed the new magazine on the pile, stating simply that it was more appropriate. It only had a shirtless man on the cover.

This would be an awakening moment for me. On the ride home, I sat in the backseat, flipping through the pages, intermittently lit by passing streetlights or cars and I found myself overwhelmed by a new set of confusing feelings. While originally, I was mesmerized by the seemingly impossible image of a superhuman man wearing women's underwear, pink underwear no less. Now my senses were flooded with confusing excitement over the images of men, otherwise engaging in normal masculine behavior.

I instantly panicked, thinking my grandparents would notice my excitement. My breathing increased, my skin flushed, and I was mortified by what I somehow knew were forbidden feelings. As soon as I got home, I hid the magazine as deeply in my closet as I could, and I only dared glance at the images when I knew I was absolutely alone. I had periods of time between the end of school and my dad and stepmother coming home from work. Those periods were carefully managed for maximum study of that magazine.

Unfortunately, I did not anticipate my grandmother relaying the story of my new discovery to my father, which she innocently did, thinking she had found a new interest of mine he would finally approve of. Without warning, my father demanded to see the magazine. I went and got it and slowly walked back, my chest was tight with anxiety, fear and anticipation, my mind was racing with all the possibilities and consequences. I drafted a dozen reasons that would seem plausible and hopefully quell his anger.

To my surprise he was pleased with what he saw. Flipping through the pages he nodded in approval and smiled at me with astonished relief. He handed it back to me and with a skip in his step left me standing in complete shock. He was happy. I looked down at the magazine and realized what I had to do. If I couldn't be like the other boys, but being a girl wasn't an option, then I just had to become a superhero. That would be the key to my father's approval and happiness.

My dad didn't realize he had accidentally validated my growing awareness of attraction to men, all he seemed to notice was I was interested in a masculine activity he very much approved of. In fact, that magazine inspired "the talk" my dad had been avoiding for some time. He walked in on me in the bathroom while I was posing like the men in the magazine and apparently was noticeably aroused.

He shut the door quickly and a few days later he approached me randomly in the hallway and with enormous discomfort, asked me if I'd had erections before. I didn't associate them with anything negative at that point, so I just nodded with confused curiosity. Was there something particularly interesting about that experience? It always seemed like a normal part of my daily routine to me.

"What, um, well...what, makes that happen to you?" he managed to ask me. With a blank stare I titled my head slightly and said, "Um, muscles?" His face instantly turned white, and this dramatic reaction altered all of my already heightened senses. "On women?" he cautiously asked. "No," I paused, "on men."

I assumed the issue had been settled. He saw the magazine. He seemed to approve of everything in it. He was constantly buying me posters of shirtless athletes, making me watch sporting events, including professional wrestling, and insisting I take my shirt off at the pool or when I played outside. I assumed all boys and men enjoyed well-built shirtless men. Why else would they keep photos of them around and stare at them all the time?

I hadn't yet connected feelings of sexual arousal with feelings of generalized excitement. I categorized it all as excitement and assumed it was perfectly normal. Muscular men excited me, I thought that was the point. Suddenly all of that went out the window and I felt my skin flush with insecurity. "That's not good..." he trailed off as he turned and walked away.

The subject never came up again, but the damage had been done. Was I not supposed to get excited by men? I knew I wasn't supposed to by women because my grandmother made that clear. So, was something wrong with me, more than what already was? I was only left with questions and a new overwhelming suspicion that something was obviously wrong, and I had a new secret to keep.

After avoiding me for several highly stressful days, he surprised me by excitedly bringing me into my room to show me a present he had spent nearly an entire paycheck on. He bought me an exercise machine. I found the machine a fascinating object of hope and possibility as I carefully followed the exercises in my magazine and adapted them to the machine.

The machine was stationary, moving only in up and down positions, but I was able to experiment with exercising without the mockery of my peers looking on and hoping I would fail. It became a nightly ritual of mine. It was the newest trend at the time, using stretchy resistance weights. Every time I sat against the chair and wrapped my hands around the handles, carefully positioning them just right, I felt empowered.

Shortly after my dad bought me the machine, I happened to catch the cover of a comic book while at the mall with him and he noticed my curiosity. The cover was of an overly muscular 1980's style hero and I was captivated by the strange combination of skintight clothing I normally associated with women's bathing suits or exercise clothes, and the aggressively muscular and masculine man frozen in an action pose.

My dad thought this was an excellent opportunity to introduce me to more manly interests and so he happily bought me a few issues, which I accepted with curious skepticism. I traced the lines and curves of the bodies in the drawings and compared them to my own rather geometric limbs and I felt compelled to do something about it.

If I could be bigger, stronger and assumably, super powered, the other boys would either respect me or at least leave me alone. Each night as I religiously performed my exercises, I fantasized about being one of the superheroes in my comic books and I fervently believed it was my only hope of escaping the torment of my school life.

If the exercises impacted my ten-year-old body in any way, I don't remember, but I was certainly not discovering any secret superpowers as quickly as I hoped. Part of my fantasy was that the X-Men, or Superman, the two comics in my new collection, would swoop in one day, recognize me as one of their own and take me away.

If I was good enough to join them, maybe they would protect me and bring me into their world and be my friends. The prospect of men in that position of power, confidence and physical impressiveness accepting me as one of their own was intoxicating and I spent hours comforting myself with stories of how it would all happen one day.

My inner conflict, however, was not so easily convinced. Along with the impossible proportions of the male figures in the comics, the female characters struck me as perfectly idealistic representations of what my dad seemed to enjoy in women.

They were strong, powerful, and strikingly beautiful and the men I longed to see smile in approval of me were constantly chasing after them. I especially connected to Rogue and Jean Grey, although Storm was my favorite. Rogue was fascinating to me because she was unable to truly connect with anyone despite being capable of absolutely anything.

I loved her story and I desperately wanted to be her friend so I could show her she wasn't alone. I felt very much like her. I too stood and watched from afar, stealing the body language and identities of those around me, trying to find just the right combination that might provide me social functionality, or at least, help me disappear into the crowd.

Jean Grey was different. She was able to use her mind to do incredible things but was also under constant threat of her powers taking over and destroying everything around her. I knew what that felt like too. Far too many times had I innocently turned in an assignment and found myself being singled out by the teacher, to the clearly annoyed and resentful faces of my peers.

My intelligence felt like a curse to me. No matter what the subject or test, I quickly understood it and completed what was asked of me and then became painfully bored. When I became bored I fidgeted and squirmed, to the endless frustration of my teachers and the constant giggling of my classmates. Being smart made me weird.

I wanted to be like Jean Grey and able to trick everyone into not being able to see me so I could go through my day without standing out. The more I tried to hide the more obvious I was, and I could never seem to escape the attention and judgement of the other kids around me.

Storm, of course, was an astonishingly beautiful goddess with pure white hair and eyes who could fly and summon lightning bolts from her fingertips. When she was sad, it became cloudy, and it rained. I too noticed that sometimes when I was sad, the clouds seemed to roll in as if to catch up with me. I often believed everything in my environment reflected either my failure or my joy.

Beyond the fantasy of superpowers, though, was the fantasy of being one of these strong and powerful women. I admired the male characters, mostly physically, and I soaked up every personality detail I could interpret from the text hoping to find just the right algorithm to incorporate into my own personality.

I especially felt sympathetic to Wolverine, a dark and brooding character who frequently flew into fits of rage only to stare at the carnage he caused and lower his head in frustrated regret. He reminded me of my father, and I thought that if I could save him, maybe I could save my dad too.

I didn't really imagine myself as one of them, though. I wanted their attention and affection and I wanted them to defend me from my bullies. I wanted to give them something they had never had before in a friend and truly, profoundly, help them. I wanted them to find me as interesting and worthy of defending as the women in their fictional lives.

The girls, however, inspired true imagination and I frequently fantasized about what being one of them would be like. I would often sink down into the bathtub until the water was just at the edges of my face and my ears were flooded, and I would focus intensely on reshaping my body to match Rogue's or Jean Grey's.

Crossing my legs, I would mimic their poses and I would stretch out my arms as high I could, watching droplets of water flow down what I hoped were graceful limbs. Under the water, my hair felt freer, and it flowed around my face, allowing me the sensation of feminine beauty.

But just as I had grown accustomed to over years of desperate pleading before falling asleep, I always had to face my reflection in the mirror when the water became too cold, and I was forced to return to my truly artificial life. I would sometimes allow my hair, when it was longer and shaggier, to remain plastered to my face so that the only glimpse of a reflection I would see would momentarily resemble the flowing beauty I pictured under the water.

At this age, I was well-known in my school for being a talented singer and performer, something that frequently shocked the adults who witnessed these events. Somehow when I was on stage I became a different person, bold, energetic, and charismatic. My grandmother also loved performing, joining choirs, and other singing groups in her social circles. It was something we often did together.

I even impressed her church choir enough to be invited to join them for their Christmas performance that year, being the only child among them. My voice was high pitched, and I could easily match the other Sopranos in the group. Even my grandfather had, at one rare point in his life, not been able to resist the bug, starring in his high school play.

My grandmother would light up in the audience watching me perform and I often performed just for her. My father rarely attended, but it didn't seem to matter because my grandparents were audience enough for me. I never grew tired of seeing her normally controlled expression widen and her steady voice raise with excitement after a performance.

She was always so proud of me, and my grandfather's typically reserved and disinterested persona would bloom as he raised his arms, smiling broadly. Due to my exuberance, I was a fan favorite of the other parents in the audience and my music teachers provided me every opportunity to sing and dance to my heart's content. Even my peers seemed impressed at times by my contagious energy.

There was an opportunity that arose at a local theater group where they needed several kids my age. The play was a comedy called, *The Best Christmas Pageant Ever*, with limited singing and no dancing, but I did manage to earn a single line. At a pivotal scene, in which I and a dozen other students pretended to be in music class, I would be poked and taunted by a girl next to me and would shout out, "She won't stop touching me!" to which the pretend teacher would intervene, giving the main character an opportunity to sneak away for his own plot line.

Other than that, I mainly stayed in the background, trying not to draw attention to myself. I believe my character also played either Joseph or a wiseman in the pretend Christmas play and I was captured in a local news article photo dressed with a towel around my head in a bathrobe.

While I did no better in that social group than I did in any other. I once stepped on the foot of my pretend teacher shortly after getting in trouble for ad-libbing lines in my one scene and distracting her. Practicing the play in its entirety with a small toy stage and my troll dolls, I felt I was obviously a better choice for the lead. Despite that disappointment and the general annoyance of my theater colleagues, it wasn't all bad. There was one huge benefit to the activity I never anticipated. I was allowed to wear makeup.

I discovered this purely by accident as my father and I were given a tour of the backstage area with the other families right before our first rehearsal. We passed through a long hallway with a wall of mirrors and a solid row of counter space covered end to end with boxes of assorted makeup and other props and accessories.

My eyes instantly lit up when I saw the makeup out in the open and caught the tour guide joking about how even the boys had to put on lipstick, to the groans of the other boys behind me. But for me this was a revelation. Boys could wear makeup? Grown men put on makeup? And this was perfectly acceptable?!

My dad was less than thrilled but lost in the moment I rushed over to a box of makeup, with the mistaken impression the guide meant I could put on makeup right there and then, and I began to scan through the multitude of options. Picking up a bright red lipstick that resembled one of my grandmother's favorite shades, I slowly twisted the tube and held my breath as the deep red symbol of possibility turned to face me.

The moment ended there, though, as the guide quickly snatched the lipstick away and laughed that I wouldn't need that much makeup. The other kids laughed, and my father frowned, but I was not discouraged. There would be a time when putting on makeup would be as normal as it was on Halloween when I was free to paint my face with abandon. That time would come soon, and I would cherish every minute of it.

And cherish it I did. Makeup was only applied for the dress rehearsals right before the public performances, but I had been eagerly anticipating it for weeks. I walked by the long table of magical paintbrushes, colorful tubes and forbidden pencils and crayons every rehearsal, and finally the day came, and my dad wasn't there to witness it.

I was dismayed that I was not permitted to freely apply the makeup to enhance my face as I saw fit as the purpose, especially for boys and men, was to simply allow normal features to be seen in bright lights. Nevertheless, I remained optimistic.

I was instructed to sit quietly and very still facing an older woman who was in charge of painting my face. Naturally she assumed I would be horrified by the entire process, so she was prepared to slather it on as quickly as possible and move on to the next disgruntled kid. I would have none of that.

I insisted she explain the purpose of every layer, every tool, every dollop of foundation and pad of blush and to my surprise she was more than happy to indulge me. I remember sitting at a slight angle so I could watch and being mesmerized by the odd sensation of her applying the strange concoctions to my face and watching it happen at the same time.

Foundation was cold, I didn't expect that. It always went on so smoothly when my grandmother put hers on. The blush and eyeshadow went by more quickly than I would have liked, and the application of eyeliner was more difficult than I anticipated, but the star of the show was the lipstick.

There is just something about putting on lipstick. I frequently pretended to do so with ChapStick, which despite being fairly common in usage for both boys and girls, was a spectacle for me. I tended to get lost in the sensation of the smooth, tingly wax, coating my lips only to indulge an exaggerated smack to apply it evenly. Apparently, it was quite the amusing sight.

"Pucker up," my makeup artist instructed, and boy did I ever. She slid the smooth, waxy color onto my lower lip, paused and then smacked her own lips to show me how to do mine. But I didn't need her help in that department. I smooshed my lips together, triumphantly shook my head and quickly turned to gaze at my reflection. Beautiful. I felt, beautiful.

I had to wash it all off before my dad came to pick me up though. He never said anything, but I felt an urgent impending shame at the thought of him seeing me dolled up in such a way. My instincts were correct, as on opening night after the performance I ran out to meet him, my stepmother, sister, and grandparents, and he frowned when he looked down at me.

"Why do they have to make you look like a girl?" he lamented, as he smudged the lipstick off my lips with his thumb. The shame was omnipresent. I never got to go home and see myself in the mirror. I always had my ChapStick though, and boy did I make up for it.

The one exception to the boy and girl color restrictions in my life was out of pure coincidence. My school colors were purple and white. From elementary school through high school, I was constantly inundated in the color purple. Despite falling squarely in the 'girl' column, when associated with school, all the rules went out the window.

Both my grandparents and both my parents went to the same school I did, and purple was a sacred color in our household. The rival school was green and white, and a further away competitor was blue and white. The three schools had been mortal enemies for generations and each designated area proudly defended their colors.

All the athletes wore purple, all the male teachers and coaches wore purple and most importantly, my father wore purple. Purple became a clever escape for me as pink easily slipping into the purple spectrum without much intrusion. Although the official school color was of a dark plum, any shade of purple was sufficient in demonstrating school spirit.

This meant I got to have a wide array of purple shades to work with. When I filled in coloring pages with purple, I could easily sneak in a few blended shades of pink in as well without detection. It was the perfect disguise. To make things even better, when school pride days did occur, everyone wore purple, including the boys. For those brief moments, I was indistinguishable between either gender divide. We were all purple.

THREE

My Grandmother's Rings

I absolutely loved women. I loved everything about them. I loved their hair, their makeup, their clothes and especially, their jewelry. My grandmother embodied all these qualities, taking care each morning to ensure every inch of her presence demonstrated sophistication and class. She had a large walk-in closet and was extraordinarily proud of her collection of matching outfits, jewelry, and purses in every color of the rainbow and for any occasion.

Like many women of her generation, she never left the house with a curl out of place or a wrinkle in her dress. On weekends when I would sometimes spend the night, she would take me into her closet and let me pick her outfit for the day. Dressed in a flowing morning gown, matching slippers and her hair carefully bundled in curlers and bobby pins, held together with a silk scarf, we would dance through her vast array of options, choosing the perfect combination of color, pattern, and style.

Far before I could remember, we engaged in this ritual, and I would watch her with absolute fascination as she carefully put on her makeup and delicately unraveled each curl. My memories involve me sitting on her covered toilet seat, which matched the rug, towels, and shower curtain, and staring up in a trance watching her apply layers of makeup. Each stroke of a brush or gentle pat of color seemed like magic to me.

The most magical moment of all, however, was when she was completely put together and ready to select her most prized possessions, her jewelry. She and my grandfather, although I never knew it, had a cold marriage and they had merely lived together for decades, long before I was even born. She had always taken care of herself, however, and was no helpless housewife.

By age fifteen she had left her abusive home, atop a mountain in the woods of Charleston, WV, where they had no running water and she taught herself to read by following the comic strips and news stories of the newspaper that acted as wallpaper in their log cabin. Her father, a drunk and a gambler, reportedly chased her down the hill firing his shotgun in her direction the day she graduated high school and got into an argument with him over his treatment of her mother.

She lied about her age and got her first job in a department store and her first apartment, a room in an elderly woman's house, which cost her seven dollars a week. Though she married my grandfather shortly after, she always worked to support him at his job at the railroad, which he began at age nineteen and ended upon retirement. She became a real estate agent at a time when the idea that a woman could sell anything was publicly laughed at and she was given the worst listings in an effort to discourage her. She became the top selling agent within a year.

She ran for office, becoming the first woman in her small town to win an election and she would go on to chair the Ohio chapter of the AARP in her retirement years. She gained her bachelor's degree, one class at a time, paid out of pocket, over years and even produced a local television show. She sang with a large group of women who toured the area performing for charity. She earned everything she ever had, and she expressed this most defiantly in her love of jewelry.

Over the years she bought herself rings, necklaces, and other assorted accessories as small rewards for her hard work. Sadly, her husband did not appreciate her beauty or her value and so if she wanted to feel special, she had to do it herself. Every piece in her collection represented a moment of affirmation, accomplishment, and satisfaction for her. Choosing which pieces to wear each day became a ritual of validation and celebration.

I often became the deciding vote between two competing pieces when shopping and I cherished the dazzling jewels speckled throughout her rows and rows of treasures that I had chosen. Sitting on the edge of her bed, she would open the doors of her large, floor-standing jewelry chest and carefully select a drawer to pull forward, revealing am array of sparkling gems, each eager to reflect her pride and beauty that day. She would choose a selection, hand them to me and I would make the final decision.

I remember holding each ring and gazing in awe as the jewels shimmered in the low light of her bedroom, creating the tiniest of reflections on the walls. I would slip the oversized golden loop over my finger and propping it up with my other hand, hold it out in front me and slowly wave my fingers back and forth. My grandmother, looking on approvingly, would gasp and giggle along with me, as we discussed the various persuasive qualities of each ring.

She could never choose just one, however, and each finger frequently displayed multiple rings. A few bracelets, a necklace or two, a perfectly matched broach and finally, a set of clip-on earrings to complete the look. Even if she had no intentions of leaving the house that day, she was ready for an interview with Barbara Walters, as she liked to say, if the occasion called for it. She was simply put, perfection.

All I wanted was to be her. I idolized her and incorporated her body language, speaking style, dry, often dark, humor, and her flair for color and opulence into my own personality. Even though she frequently gushed to others of my blue eyes, I longed for deep brown eyes like hers. As my hair grew darker and redder over time, I lamented how much contrast there was between it and her platinum blonde curls. She even dyed my hair on occasion to relieve my dissatisfaction and to indulge her own fantasy of my being the perfect blue-eyed, blonde-haired boy, despite those nasty hints of ginger she so despised.

She frequently tested out a nail color on me as well, before committing to it herself. She did have ten fingers and ten toes to think of. I would hold my hand out in front of me, smiling gleefully at the single square of bright red or fuchsia glimmering back at me and for a moment I felt so glamorous and free. She was sure to remove any trace of it before I went home for the evening, and I always had the strongest sense of guilt and shame associated with the ritual.

When I was with her, I could be myself. Lacking a childhood of her own, she indulged herself with dollhouses and miniatures. We would sit on the floor and play with her dollhouse, telling each other stories and rearranging the scenes as needed. When she was a little girl, she dedicated most of her time to caring for her younger brothers while her older sister ventured out on her own, marrying her first husband at age fourteen.

Her youngest brother, who would later marry her best friend and become her pastor, was nearly killed when walking the streets of Charleston, WV, he grabbed a downed power line attempted to reenact Tarzan. She felt a deep sense of obligation to care for her siblings, and on more than one occasion she mistakenly called me one of her younger brother's names instead of my own.

She was extremely intelligent, skipping multiple grades in her country school where she sat with older students, learning far beyond her assigned grade. Still, she never truly got to be a child. She longed for a doll house to indulge her fantasies of a happy family, but her parents could never afford such things.

She loved to tell me of a story where several older boys convinced her and her brothers that they had seen a huge, gorgeous doll house in the local landfill. Convincing her brothers to come with her, they traveled to the landfill and spent the next several hours diligently searching every square inch of trash until her dreams were crushed by the mischievous boys laughing at them from atop a trash heap.

From that day on she vowed to one day have a beautiful, full and intricate doll house of her very own. It took her several decades, but she finally made her dream come true, finding one that stood three feet or so tall and wide, which she displayed on a table and delighted in discovering new miniatures to fill it with.

One of my favorite hunting adventures in stores was to try and find her something unique for her doll house. Whatever she couldn't find, she made herself. She had even created tiny replicas of common things like boxes of cereal by copying the front and back on a black and white copier and progressively shrinking them down until she could glue them into a tiny box.

I fully and truly believed she was magical, and she was happy to keep the fantasy alive by playing a game where she had me close my eyes and she would disappear right outside the door, and I would be convinced she had turned herself into a doll sitting within the tiny house. She would then talk to me in a smaller voice, trying not to break character seeing my astonished reaction. She had a small Barbie replica she got from a Happy Meal from McDonald's at one point, that she made a tiny dress for to go over the painted-on original. She hid the doll and would quickly slip it into the house when my eyes were closed.

I inherited her doll house and her complete collection of miniatures. Although over time, the house itself slowly crumbled, I still have many of the pieces she treasured inside. Her tiny doppelganger was reborn as my cat Freddie's favorite toy, however. He would carry her around by the hair in his mouth and snuggle up with her whenever he took a nap. I was forever finding the thing under my pillow or tucked behind my back. When Freddie passed, he was put to rest with his favorite toy in the world.

Her love of miniatures became a mutual obsession and I still find myself fixated on any I come across, admiring their tiny details, and imagining how much my grandmother would have loved it. Her creativity was not always appreciated by her family, but she made so much of my childhood magical. She convinced me we had a family of fairies in the backyard as well, carefully placing tiny shoes or a table set at the foot of a blooming Dogwood tree for me to find early on a Saturday morning.

I searched for those fairies for years. Only she had seen them, which was evidence enough for me. My father would frown in disappointment when I told him of my fairy hunting adventures earlier that day. But with my grandmother I was safe. I knew I couldn't be a girl, but at least at my grandmother's house, I didn't have to try so hard to be a boy.

My grandmother loved dresses and in turn, so did I. She would always show off her outfit for me after putting it on, twirling out of her closet and finishing with a dramatic pose, only to lose her composure with laughter. As a girl she had dreamed of being an actress in Hollywood, rubbing elbows with the stars and getting to wear the most beautiful of gowns and the most expensive jewelry.

She frequently referenced Elizabeth Taylor and how she was always dripping with diamonds. She absolutely idolized her and had photos of her on the wall. In many ways she and I were very much alike, forced to gaze through the window of fantasy to enjoy lives we would never be allowed to live.

She had collected her clothing over decades, and it didn't seem to matter if the outfit was purchased forty years prior or just that weekend, she wore it as though she had designed it herself. Every outing was an opportunity to dazzle and impress and she never missed a single one.

For me, seeing her so poised and so glamorous, I could only imagine how wonderful it would be to have a life like hers. I thought she was rich and famous well into my early teen years. She seemed to know everyone, had connections to the highest political contacts in the country and you would think she was a retired movie star from the way she carried herself.

I didn't just want to be like her, I needed to be. Never one to tiptoe around difficult subjects, I knew of her childhood and her heroics early on. She shared her stories with me as though we were sisters, and I was the only one she could trust in the world.

Her stories were always purposeful, though, and they held an important lesson. I took them all in and would drift to sleep imagining them in great detail. If she could become the iconic beauty she was, having lived through so much difficulty and suffering, so could I.

I watched her day after day in her stunning clothes, usually covered in rhinestones or sequins, and I reasoned that she was the living embodiment of strength and survival. Whereas my grandfather typically lived in slacks and a white undershirt, only putting on a button-up, short-sleeved shirt when necessary and my dad never seemed to be wearing anything other than sweatpants and a tucked-in T-shirt, my grandmother owned her presence in a way that inspired me.

Men had to restrain their personal style, but women could exploit it to the fullest extent. The more a woman accessorized with glitter, jewels, and beautiful, flowing silk, the more empowered and joyful she was. Men were boring, but women could be inspiring. But only if they were special enough to know it.

I hated my own clothes. Everything I owned was blue or green with an occasional yellow or red in the mix. I seemed to only wear shorts and polo shirts. My grandmother made sure I looked presentable alongside her, but my dad certainly didn't care what I looked like. My stepmother was perpetually in oversized summer dresses, often referred to as muumuus.

My sister too was as casual as one could be, living mostly in shorts and T-shirts, only wearing dresses on the rarest of occasions and with great protest. She was tomboy and I hated her for it. I couldn't even sneak into her room to steal anything interesting. She usually wore my hand-me-downs.

To add to the desert of opportunity for secret feminine indulgence, my stepmother was strictly anti-makeup. She grew up in a severe religious household and despite a wild period in college, she had largely resigned herself to long dresses and her waist-length hair kept up in a perpetual bun.

There was, however, one night where her younger wild self surfaced and she brought me along for the ride. My father was working for the night, it was Friday evening, and it was just my stepmother, my sister and myself and we decided to watch *Grease* on VHS.

In an unusually good mood that evening, she had a wide smile that lit up her face, something I rarely saw, and she danced, waving her arms out of rhythm and sang off-key, trying her best to make us both join in and laugh. I loved *Grease* and I knew all the songs by heart, and so I greedily took advantage of her gregarious mood and only my sister stared on in baffled disbelief.

At a key point in the movie, when the main characters sing a lively duet, she paused the movie and ran to her room, emerging wearing a new skirt and heels. I don't know what came over me, but I asked if I too could put on a skirt and heels and insisted my sister do the same.

Shouting, "hurry," my sister and I ran to her room, and I nearly tripped over myself with excitement. I grabbed a long skirt and quickly pulled it up over my shorts and then slide my right foot into a slightly too-small heel, pausing for a moment to take in the absurdity, and then put on the other. My sister did the same.

We entered the living room, dressed alike, and my stepmother pulled us both up onto the blocky wooden living room table and resumed the movie. In an instant we were all three holding hands and dancing in a circle, trying not to fall off the table. Only I managed to maintain my balance and for a moment I was on stage, in a dress and in heels, tap dancing to "You Better Shape Up" and singing along with Olivia Newton John as they both giggled on the floor looking up at me.

It was utterly euphoric. I was bursting with laughter and sharing the moment with two people I normally avoided interaction with, and it was wonderful. I had thrown caution to the wind and the risk paid off and my god it was remarkable. The sensation of pure ecstatic abandon, with the feel and sound of heels on that blocky wooden table, holding up my skirt as to not fall, it was all so magical.

And then headlights broke through the curtains, shining a spotlight on me, standing on the table, in a skirt and heels. My stepmother, frozen in fear, whispered for us to quickly go to our rooms before my father could open the door. It was too late.

He had seen everything through the window and the transparency of the curtains against a blackened backdrop of night. As the door handle turned, I launched myself off of the table, running down the hall and hearing the door open and my father's angry voice shouting, I tripped and hit my head on the corner baseboard where the two pieces formed a sharp angle.

Dizzy, disoriented and feeling sick, the wave of desperate fear was replaced with a dissociative state where I found myself observing the scene, but unable to move or control it. He had grabbed my stepmother by the hair and brutally thrown her to the ground, he caught my sister by the back of her shirt pulling her backwards and tossing her to the ground next to her mother.

But his target was me. I heard his angry stomps coming toward me and enraged ranting I barely understood. I couldn't move. I was on the floor with my head bleeding and my body simply wouldn't function. I was helpless. The moment of separation was abruptly ended when he grabbed me by the back of the neck, lifted me up and slammed me against the wall.

Demanding to know what was going on, he scanned me up and down, ripping off the skirt and holding it to my face. I remember his eyes were like black voids and his face a deep red. I once again lost awareness, feeling myself fall away as my body went limp.

He dropped me to the floor, marched back into the living where my stepmother was cowering, holding onto her daughter, and he simply walked back out the door and drove away. The screeching of his tires sent chills through my body, sufficient to give me strength enough to crawl away to my bedroom.

On the baseboard, at the corner of the hall, is a dent where my head landed. My grandmother owned the house and would eventually live there again, remodeling nearly everything but that back area. She never noticed the dent and therefore never had it fixed. Whenever I visited and had reason to go to the back rooms, one of which had been my own, I would glance down at that permanent mark. The last time I gazed down that hallway in my mid-20's, after my grandmother passed and I knew I would never return there again, it was still there, reminding me that even when wounds heal, the scar never goes away

FOUR

Uncle Vince

My stepmother's family lived in Virginia, a very long trip from my home, and during my tenth summer my father surprised me one morning by announcing I would be spending my summer vacation with my stepfamily. Shortly after I was sitting in the car, staring out at a large open field filled with excited children rushing away from their parents to a central tent.

I had been taken to a summer camp, where I would be spending several weeks while my father took a vacation from his family. This was my worst nightmare come true, being forced into an unfamiliar setting with a hundred or so kids I didn't know and left to live with them without a single reassuring comfort from home.

I was unbearably hot and muggy; the camp was out in the woods without any permanent structures at the end of a long dirt road. It was a church camp and my parents decided it would be a good opportunity for me to learn good social skills.

I remember the entire experience like a dream. I got out of the car at my father's impatient command and slowly walked towards the large tent where the other children were happily frolicking, and I scanned my surroundings with terrified hyperawareness.

My memory pauses there and awakens in an old, converted school bus where I was sleeping on a blanket as far against the back wall as I could reach as dozens of other boys my age chattered and played all around me. No adults were in sight. It was dark and I could hear the deafening roar of the woods outside the windows.

It was hot, sticky, and uncomfortable. My head was next to an old bolt that once secured a seat, and I kept bumping into it as I tried to sleep. The other boys joked that a family of skunks had used the bus as a home before everyone arrived. I was silent and in shock and utterly miserable.

But something happened on that adventure that I never quite expected. Within a few days, the other kids had begun exclusively calling me, "Turner," and in their thick Virginian accent, loudly demanded I join them in their activities. Strangely, I did. Watching as though I was separated from my own body, I felt as if an entirely new person took over and decided to make the best of the situation, he knew I could never enjoy. Helpless I faded in and out, still feeling a profound sense that nothing was real, and I must be dreaming. But inside, it was remarkable and even fun.

My sister was also at the camp, and she still laughs at how astonishingly different I was there. I roughhoused with the boys, played sports, explored the woods, got dirty, freely jumped in the lake on a tire swing and seemed to be having a genuinely amazing time.

While most of the details have been lost to me, what I remember was the feeling of finally being included and accepted. No one there seemed to notice or think anything was wrong with me at all. It was as if this was how it always should have been. I also quickly adopted their accent, which was a more exaggerated version of one many kids in my own school carried, but drastically far removed from my own. It felt natural, freeing, almost like it was the real me coming out and the accent and new name were simply part of a new me.

The weeks flew by, and I remember seeing my dad arrive and running to him excitedly babbling too fast to be understood, in my new accent, all the wonderful experiences I had. For the first time in a while, he smiled down at me and seemed genuinely pleased.

I liked being Turner, and I didn't want it to end. I can still remember the feeling of strangely loving the thick, heavy summer air, and even now when I walk out on a balmy summer night and see fireflies sparkling around me, I remember that feeling.

It was that summer that I met my uncle Vince. My stepmother had an older sister and a younger brother, and he lived with his parents. He was probably in his early to mid-twenties at the time I think, and I was instantly fascinated with him. He was handsome, tall, had a good build and a warm smile which he freely offered me upon my first meeting. I always appreciated when adults acknowledged me rather than simply treating me as a kid. Another fascinating quality of his, though, was that he was deaf.

My stepmother was nearly deaf, requiring a hearing aid and she spoke with a heavy speech impediment and frequently signed as she went along. She and her brother had gotten sick with the measles when they were very young and he lost his hearing entirely, whereas she was only partially disabled.

I was intensely interested in sign language and understanding how this pure form of communication worked so fluidly. Because Vince was deaf, and my stepmother didn't get a hearing aid until her adult years, the family spoke almost exclusively in signs. It was shocking to me upon first experience, coming into the house while everyone was speaking normally and then abruptly forming a little circle with energetic flails of their hands, assisted with lip-syncing and only the faintest of mumbled words underneath.

My dad stood awkwardly by, and my sister seemed completely oblivious, but I was fascinated. I watched every moment trying to decode the language, and I thought if I could learn it, I could have a secret way of talking with my new role model, my uncle Vince.

Vince went out of his way to spend time with me, seeing me uncomfortably alone in their country home where the nearest neighbor was a mile away and they had no TV. He would approach me, carefully tapping me on the shoulder and signing to me with emphatic lip movements, hoping I would understand him. Frankly I was too overwhelmed that a man like him was talking to me at all pay attention.

He was patient, however, and didn't seem to mind repeating himself for my benefit. We spent hours together as he occupied my time with inventive ways of teaching me how to communicate with him. He would sign a sentence, say the sentence with a heavily distorted drone and then take my hand and move them to mimic the sentence. When I stared at him helplessly, he would take a marker and draw out a picture. He was determined to teach me, and he didn't give up by just writing out what he wanted to say. I had to figure it out on my own.

One facet of his way of signing was that visually it looked very much like the feminine hand gestures I was so frequently mocked for producing. When he did it though, it looked like dancing. His arms moved so gracefully and with such speed, I couldn't take in the beauty of it all at once, resigned to follow only one hand at a time.

It was this level of comfort with me and, I am guessing, the more flamboyant interaction that raised my father's suspicions. I didn't know it at the time, but Vince was gay. My dad knew it though and he was very uncomfortable with leaving me alone with him, believing he would influence me in some way.

In fact, later on when I was outed to him, he aggressively pulled me aside and demanded to know if Vince had done anything to me or taught me to be this way. He was even convinced our secret language was Vince trying to indoctrinate me without anyone knowing.

Interestingly, my stepmother's older sister was also gay and lived with a woman who was largely indistinguishable from a man. I had absolutely no idea she wasn't a man until my father pointed it out after meeting the two. Although I never heard the word "gay," and it I honestly didn't connect my aunt and her girlfriend as being anything more than friends, I was struck by the fact that outside of my world at home, adults seemed to break all the rules of gender I was being forced to live by.

My aunt and her girlfriend were very masculine women and the contrast between them, and my own grandmother was profound. I found myself studying the two, trying to understand how women could behave like, look like and dress like men so easily. Vince was flamboyant himself, with a wide, welcoming smile and bright eyes. He moved with a gracefulness I hadn't seen in other men before, and he was entirely unselfconscious about it. My dad frequently grumbled that he acted like a girl, and I found that inspiring.

He was otherwise a good looking, confident young man and yet he was also feminine and comfortable being so. My aunt and her girlfriend were the same, but even more boldly. It absolutely changed everything I thought I understood about what growing up could be like and how I might fit in.

Vince exercised every day and in my week with him, he taught me how to correctly do pushups, sit-ups and other exercises and I would do them at his side. In so many ways it was what I had always wanted. An older brother who was invested in me and enjoyed spending time with me.

He was protective of me as well, frequently stepping in when his mother snapped at me. She didn't like me at all. From the moment I met her, I found her to be cold, harsh, and frightening. She had a perpetually sour look on her face and was seemingly forever shrieking at me for doing something incorrectly.

My stepmother's family was more robust in their communication than I was used to. They would stand in a circle and their signing would become more and more exaggerated and aggressive, often breaking out into very intimidating body language and facial expressions. They seemed to be fighting, yet they were just talking.

The only kind face in the room was Vince, who would often catch me staring out of the corner of his eye and turn, smiling and performing an exaggerated eyeroll or shoulder shrug, waving away his family members as if it was nothing to worry about. He always made me feel better and safe.

It would be the last I ever saw of him, though. I didn't know it at the time, but he suffered from schizophrenia and was taking medication, which he frequently stopped taking. When he did, he would become unpredictable, violent, and paranoid. I learned as a teenager that shortly after I met him, he had been hospitalized.

My dad used his illness as a weapon to try and scare me out of being gay, insisting Vince had been locked away for that precise sin. As he saw it, being gay was what caused Vince to "go crazy" in the first place.

But before any of that, all I had was that single remarkable week to bring home with me. Alone in my room I would practice my sign language in the mirror, being as expressive and flamboyant as I wanted to be and imagining my uncle Vince there with me, laughing along and approving of my progress.

For a time, I even insisted I be called Vincent, deciding that the change was a brand-new start for me. My dad, who originally called me "Nicky" as a small child and was forever annoyed that I apparently refused to accept the change in name, was poorly amused.

However, as with many things, he decided it was merely a phase and tolerated it for a while. The change was more profound in me than anyone would have expected though. I fell into a deep depression, finding myself becoming obsessed with wanting Vince in my life all the time and wanting to go back to visit him.

At home, I was alone again. I did the exercises he taught me, but it wasn't the same. My room felt cold and empty. During my stay,

I slept in his room on the floor next to his bed, the only space available in the small country house, and the sound of him snoring was strangely comforting.

Now in my room the nights felt too silent. I just wanted to be with him, the only man I had ever met that seemed to understand me and accept me just as I was. I believed I could learn so much from him and that he could finally help me escape my torment and being separated from him was an even more cruel and frustrating reality.

I also grew to hate my own hearing. Vince was deaf and I reasoned that the only way I could ever truly be in his world was to be deaf too. Maybe if I became deaf, it would separate me from the world I could never fit in and allow me to be a part of a new one. He and I would have our own secret language and no one, especially my father, would be able to understand us. It was perfect.

I replaced my nightly prayers to wake up as a girl with a new plea to wake up without my hearing. Each morning I would slowly awaken and for a moment hold my breath to see if any sounds were perceptible. The second this was confirmed, I would sigh and stare up at the ceiling in frustration, often crying with anger.

Why couldn't I have this one thing that would change my life forever? If I was deaf, I thought, it would put a permanent barrier between my father and myself, maybe my stepmother would be happier to be around me and the kids at school would leave me alone. Then I could talk with Vince fully, without the barrier of translation and speaking. I would be able to understand the world the way he did and finally have a place in it. It became an obsession.

I tried covering my ears to muffle out the sound. I used earplugs, playdough, cotton balls, anything I thought would work. Nothing erased the sound though, not completely. Still calling myself Vincent, I resorted to willing myself to be deaf by pretending not to hear anything, something no one in my daily life was very patient with.

I even tried to convince the nurse at school who performed our annual hearing and vision tests that I couldn't hear the beeping sound in the machine so she would tell everyone I was actually losing my hearing.

In a final act of desperation, I sat in my room, holding a sharp pencil, crying and ranting to myself at how nothing in my life seemed to be fair. I had heard a million times the warnings of sharp objects near your ears, and I decided it would be the only way.

I held the pencil to my right ear, my hand shaking, and I slowly pushed it into my ear canal, until I felt a sharp pain. I stopped, instinctively pulling the pencil back out. I tried again, this time closing my eyes and preparing for a sudden, violent jab, one that would hurt, but would be over quickly.

The sharp tip entered my ear once more and with my breath tightly held in my chest, I jabbed the pencil in as hard as I could. The pain was instantaneous and terrifying, and I let out an involuntary scream. Moments later my father and stepmother burst through my door seeing me sobbing on the floor, with my head hidden by my hands and blood pouring from my ear where the pencil was still lodged.

My dad flew into a rage the moment we were home from the emergency room. He blamed Vince and blamed my stepmother for indulging my interest in sign language. It would all stop that night. I would stop calling myself Vincent, I would stop learning sign language and I would stop idolizing "that faggot."

Devastated, I felt the only hope I had left evaporate away. Although I recovered, without any hearing loss, I had to wear a large bandage on my right side, and it certainly did nothing to help me go unnoticed at school. I heavily withdrew and stopped talking or responding to anyone.

In my private moments, I still signed to myself and fantasized about Vince showing up at my house to rescue me and living out in the country, spending our days exercising, laughing, and communicating with our secret language. I still called myself Vincent on occasion when I felt the most depressed and defeated.

The night I came home from the hospital, I crawled into bed and listened to my father shouting at my stepmother, hearing his demands that I would never again have access to the person I truly believed was my salvation. Rolling over on my left side and burying my head into my pillow, though, for a short while, all sound was gone. I found peace even in that moment of deeply profound pain.

Vince, I would later learn, had developed such a strong personality because his family had been so restrictive and judgmental of who he was. He loved to send his mother into rages over his homosexuality, flaunting it to her and mocking her with it. He was under her official care, however, due to his psychological illness and he wasn't allowed to leave.

He would frequently run away, on foot, and hitch rides to bigger cities in the state, where his good looks and charm kept him under a roof and fed. He would inevitably be found though and brought back, with the threat of institutions hanging over his head. His schizophrenia was a demon that never left his side, and he was more often than not willing to indulge it.

Shortly after my visit, he got into another argument with his mother, pushing her down the basement stairs. This led to his arrest and finally, his being placed into an institution where he would later end his own life.

I was always so baffled by this story, and I wasn't told he had committed suicide until years after the fact. How could such a bright, beautiful soul be taken into such a dark place and left to finally burn out completely? His family believed the devil had taken him and he was possessed by a demon, quite literally. When I was eventually outed, my stepmother insisted that same demon had taken over me.

As I entered my second decade, I too would find myself haunted by a demon that would nearly take my life as well. When I turned 11, I tried to kill myself. As is true of so many of my memories, this one is pieced together from the stories of the people who were there and my own disjointed, disassociated perspective.

I do remember coming home from an extraordinarily horrible day at school, my cheeks sore from crying. I shuffled towards my front door, unlocked it and entered the empty and quiet house. The house was always so surreal at this time of day, the only period in which I was alone there. The air seemed to be static in place and I alone disturbed it.

Long ago, I had taken my favorite stuffed animal, named Puppy, the last gift my mother had given me, and cut a length into the back of his neck. I would hide things there that I desperately never wanted my father to find, although I cannot remember what. I would sew him back up, then cut him back open again.

I still have him and the last roughly handsewn line has become a scar, one that transports me back when I run my finger down the length of it, but not quite enough to remember. Puppy also had a necklace I made from old wire I found and a small key, situated to face the back underneath his removable jacket. I don't know what that key ever went to, but it must have been very important.

I found myself wandering aimlessly through the house, my eyes hurting, and my vision blurred. I stared out the back window to the river and I believed in that moment there was nothing more for me to fight for. I had lost the only person I thought could help me, God was ignoring me, I had been forbidden from seeing my grandmother in a petty family dispute and the cruelty of my peers was simply too much.

My dad was always being prescribed medications of some sort, often pain medications, and he the cabinet above the stove was bursting. In a secret meeting with my grandmother, she asked me to find out what medications my dad was on, believing his sudden hostility towards her was the result of him being heavily drugged.

I had stolen a bottle of something and hidden it inside Puppy, giving it to her to help in her investigation and then taking it back when she was confident in her findings. I had forgotten to put the medicine back and my father never noticed.

I remembered, however, and in a zombie-like state, shambled to my room to retrieve my beloved best friend. I begin to remember less and less, as it felt like I was no longer in control of my body at all and apparently, I took a large number of pills. My dad discovered me crumpled on my grandparent's deck next door, unconscious.

My grandmother, as she would tell me later, and my grandfather had left to go to a church conference several hours away. If they had been home, they would have seen me and acted sooner. Fortunately, it wasn't too late and at the emergency room they were able to pump my stomach.

I woke up some time later in a hospital bed, alone, and believing I had either gone to hell for killing myself or had been institutionalized like my Uncle Vince. That's all I remember and soon I was home again, and everyone was carefully monitoring everything I did. I could no longer have my door closed. I couldn't venture out on my own or go down to the riverbank. I just sat on the couch watching TV, not speaking, and wished more than anything I had never woken up.

FIVE

Losing My Faith

At age eleven my world turned upside down. For a few years since my father remarried, I had suffered not only physical and psychological abuse from him, but also from her. They married because she thought her daughter needed a father and he thought I needed a mother. The benefit of two incomes couldn't hurt either. But neither of them felt much for one another. My dad subsequently took on three jobs, one full time during the day and two part time jobs throughout the week, not including his volunteer work at the fire department which he had been doing since he was a teenager.

With a new mother around, my grandmother decided to limit our visits to weekends so I could finally, hopefully, experience a normal and functioning family. She didn't much care for my stepmother and found my new, younger stepsister to be a nightmare to handle. But she hoped so much of what I lacked could be fulfilled. My stepmother, feeling trapped in an unhappy and lonely marriage and resentful of the attention my grandparents gave me while tangibly rejecting her daughter, took her frustrations out on me.

My new sister was biracial, and her father had left them while my stepmother was still pregnant. My grandmother's cultural sensibilities could not tolerate such a situation, having protected her reputation from tarnishing by explaining my own mother's sudden disappearance as her untimely death. My grandfather would not even allow my sister into his house, referring to her with the most forbidden of racial slurs and both were terrified their small community might imagine their son had engaged in an illicit affair with a black woman.

As a result, my stepmother frequently and vocally protested my involvement with my grandparents at all, despite living next door and in the house my father rented from them. She was also mentally unwell, suffering from bipolar disorder, and being almost entirely deaf, in a constant state of paranoia of what my father and his mother were plotting against her. When I tried to learn sign language to better communicate with her, she thought I was mocking her. We fought almost every day.

It was when my father was away that she unleashed the full force of her wrath onto me, beating me with incoherent shouting and hysterical screams. Often without warning she would erupt in rage, screaming with wild flails, leaving me in a baffled, sobbing ball on the floor. Fiercely protective of her daughter, she would launch into violent outbursts at the slightest accusation and my sister soon learned to use this to her advantage.

I still have the scars on my back from her strikes with a belt that had a large metal buckle. I would often go days without being allowed dinner or to use the bathroom. When my grandmother remodeled the house, they found the spot inside my closet where I frequently relieved myself in secret for years.

The teachers at school soon noticed. But my loyalty to my father blinded me to the danger I was in, and I insisted nothing was wrong, until I could no longer hold it inside. One day during gym after several boys cornered me and launched a brutal attack with dodgeballs as I lay helpless on the floor, I finally exploded in hysterical rage.

I shouted through tears in a long string of unbroken sentences the pain and violence I was suffering. As the boys backed away looking on in baffled surprise, I fell to the floor in utter defeat, pleading for them, and everyone to stop hurting me. They didn't laugh that day. They didn't mock me or taunt me further. They just backed away as teachers pulled them away and surrounded me. One noticed my back from my disheveled clothing and saw the deep, red slashes.

Within a month I was standing before a judge. Ashamed and afraid, I stood in a grey suit, the same one I wore to my father's wedding, and told the room what had happened to me. My mother, standing next to me, a new source of comfort in my life, provided encouragement with slight squeezes of her hand on my shoulder.

I walked out of the courtroom, now in the custody of my mother, based on my own testimony and decision, and when I tried to hug my dad for the last time, he pulled away, refusing to look at me. I stared, motionless and silent for the thirteen-hour trip to Florida, where I would be starting a new life. My grandmother had been taken from me twice, my grandfather was devastated and increased his drinking, I am told. Soon they would divorce, no longer feeling obligated to stay together for my sake.

I had another sister, one separated from me at a very early age, one I believed had died, and she was not my enemy, as my other sister had chosen to be. After several weeks of silence, she managed to bring me out of my shocked state and began to help me find a new version of myself. Upon my arrival, the new family I had waiting had been extremely concerned about me. I had stopped speaking. I stayed almost exclusively in a trance-like state. Psychology recognizes this as disassociation after trauma.

I have very little memory of this time, experiencing my father pulling away from me, and then feeling little but numb nothingness afterwards. It surprises me to hear how I remained like this for weeks as it didn't feel that long to me. But slowly I adapted to my new surroundings, my new cousins, all around my age, my new sister and having a mother, one I had long age mourned as dead. Like the heat of Florida, it took my breath away every day, but eventually, I got used to the storms.

The first order of action for my new parents was to address my crippling depression. My mother accidentally came upon me sitting in a room alone playing with one of my sister's Barbie dolls. Rather than interrupt me, she, my stepfather, and my sister later went to the store, and she let me pick one out for myself.

A little while prior, during a special trip to McDonald's, she noticed that I traded my sister for her Barbie doll Happy Meal toy, a pink and gold plastic replica with a modest amount of brushable blonde hair that was strikingly similar to the one my grandmother used to represent herself.

The experience was exhilarating. I hadn't even been allowed to venture down that isle before and suddenly I was being escorted by adults, my mother, and told I could pick one out for myself? I cried, overwhelmed with the weight of the experience, I collapsed unable to control the flow of tears and we quickly left the store, but not before my stepfather grabbed one of the dolls to take with us. For weeks after I still hid in my closet to play with her, afraid that I would cross some invisible line and be rejected by my new parents.

They seemed to accept my femininity, however, and soon I was testing more and more barriers, singing to Disney movies, dancing around with my sister and even wearing some of my sister's clothing. But as the summer came to an end and I had to begin a new school year, the pressure and fear returned. I had gone to school with the same hundred or so kids my entire life up until that point. Now I would be alone in a new environment filled with hundreds I had never met.

My one secure foundation came in the form of a church my new parents began taking me to shortly after I arrived. It was different from the church I grew up in, a bit livelier, and there were more kids my age. There was one kid, however, that stood out. His name was Andy, and he was older by a few years. He was the pastor's son and on one of my first visits, he noticed I was sitting alone, and he came over and sat next to me.

He was unlike any other boy I had ever met. He had long blonde hair, shaved up to his temples and pulled back into a ponytail. He was gregarious, open, friendly, and affectionate. He often hugged me when he saw me or put his arm around me during services and pulled me against him protectively. He had taken it upon himself to take care of me and he soon became my best friend.

Ironically, my family was living in the same house he had lived in shortly before and I slept in his bedroom. There was a sticker on the ceiling fan of an anarchist A, and I stared up at it imagining him and his secret life in that same room. I had never had a male friend before. No other boy had ever been nice to me, let alone protective of me. I would quickly find myself falling deeply into puppy love.

The church became my safe place where I was accepted and even celebrated. One of my most annoying characteristics was that I was smart. I always got the highest grades and always quickly understood new concepts in class, leaving me bored and restless. If I didn't already stand out for my feminine behavior and my anti-social weirdness, my constant high performance in class made me no friends. I frequently tried doing poorly just so I wouldn't be called out by the teacher for being the best.

But suddenly my intelligence and my academic interest in religious study were viewed as impressive and important. Being so young and able to keep up with adult discussions of complex Bible topics made me popular with the adults who encouraged their kids to spend time with me. At church I was popular and appreciated, and Andy was there.

For a time, my desperation over gender subsided and I found a niche where I didn't have to be a boy or a girl. It didn't seem to matter. I could freely be friends with girls, the boys were mostly introspective, polite, outcasts in their own social circles and, well, Andy was there. It gave me something to look forward to every Sunday and every Wednesday. No matter how difficult my week had been, I knew Andy's smiling face and welcoming hug would make it ok.

Part of the custody agreement was that I had to see a therapist routinely and I didn't trust therapists. I had seen them before, when I was younger than seven, after my suicide attempt and then consistently through to when I was taken from my father. I displayed worrying characteristics thought to be early signs of schizophrenia. I frequently dissociated and would be found silently staring without responding only to suddenly awaken and not remember what I had been doing.

I had suffered some kind of severe damage to my lower intestines when I was five or six, and I responded with terrified hysteria when I was touched. I was constantly being evaluated by doctors. I refused to be left alone with any man that wasn't my father or my grandfather and I frequently hid rectal bleeding that would only be discovered from bedsheets or my underwear later. Despite my high performance in school, I was inconsistent with my mood, repeatedly used other names and had a high frequency of memory loss.

My father had been ashamed of all this, I am told, and my grandmother had worked specifically with my school administrators to cover my behavior whenever necessary, including removing me from class or taking me into the women's bathroom. My grandfather's brother, who had a reputation for getting teenage boys drunk at his house, he was the fire chief and apparently abused his authority quite often, watched me during that time period. He was suddenly pulled from my life, and I was forbidden to be near him.

I would often be found sitting alone staring off into the distance or talking to someone else, only to stop, turn slowly to meet the eyes of the teacher interrupting me and suddenly awaken and begin to panic, unaware of where I was. Each therapist I saw diagnosed me with something different and I was placed on multiple medications. But nothing ever seemed to help. I quickly learned to better hide as to not draw attention from adults.

This new therapist, however, was different. He was friendly, he was handsome, he was young, and he seemed to understand me. I quite fondly remember our sessions together, but all that changed when one day after a session, I noticed my mother had left out a folder on the table she brought from the office. It had my name on it and I opened it, it was therapist notes about me, and I was horrified by what I read.

One evening my parents sat me down and talked with me in an odd interview style, getting me to open up about all kinds of things I didn't normally talk about. My magazine, which I always kept securely in my room, had traveled with me and my new parents weren't as optimistic about it as my father had been. It seems, I was being recorded and the tape along with the magazine had been given to my new doctor.

I had never noticed him taking notes before during our sessions, but I felt betrayed that what we talked about was not only written down but given to my parents. The language was so cold, and I remember feeling a sinking sensation in my stomach as I read over what this man, a man I trusted, thought of me. Although most of the discussion was surrounding abuse, disassociation, psychosis, delusions, depression and so on, one word stood out the most, homosexual.

I had no idea what it was, but I was described as being one. Strangely I felt the word was familiar, and I remembered seeing in the Bible, I thought. So, I looked in the index, and there it was, and the passages related were strikingly disturbing. I was shaken, deeply, and I simply could not understand what it all meant. All I knew was that apparently, I was one and God did not think highly of us.

As soon as I could I approached my pastor and I asked him what the word meant, after he avoided the question a few times, I insisted and pointed out that I might be one, to which he looked at me with severe eyes and said simply, "It isn't good." My horror deepened instantly, and I spiraled into a haunting despair that I was somehow something God despised and even my pastor couldn't, or wouldn't, help me.

When my parents discovered I had read the notes, they decided it was best for me to talk to someone who could better explain it to me. So, they reached out to a friend who was gay and asked him to talk with me. I was twelve by this time, and at first it was very comforting to know that I wasn't the only one. He insisted it was normal and that I was born that way and he also insisted I accept that I would never be able to be the Christian I wanted to me or grow up to live the live I assumed I would. Instead, I would be free from social and moral restrictions on sex and relationships, and I would be able to live whatever life I wanted. To demonstrate this to me, he showed me porn from his collection.

What would follow would become one of the most difficult experiences of my life to live with. I found myself infatuated with him because he talked to me like I was an adult. His body language was open, and I felt like I was with a secret friend that could teach me the mysteries of the world no other kid my age was privy to. I trusted him implicitly.

So, when he told me I had to learn how to perform certain actions for men if I wanted to be accepted, loved and popular, and then exposed himself to me, I believed he was doing what was best, considering what I now was. For months he escalated the encounters, making me promise to keep it a secret and to recognize how lucky and special I was to be treated by an adult in such a way. Despite feeling overwhelmed with guilt that conflicted with excitement and the intoxicating thrill of acceptance and belonging, I secretly cried myself to sleep every night.

After a year, he suddenly vanished from my life and I was devastated, believing I had somehow failed him, and he had abandoned me. I couldn't talk about what happened because I promised not to. I was alone again; except this time, I no longer had my faith to support me. I began obsessing over every possible angle of religious teaching I could find. I knew that unless I met another man like him to accept me, I would be alone forever, and God had abandoned me.

Andy had a girlfriend, and in a year's time had grown out of his interest in church activities, only showing up when forced to by his father. He had become distant, angry, and well, a teenager. I realized I had two choices, if I could be a girl then Andy or someone like Andy, would love me. The other was to do the things the man I trusted taught me to do in order to earn love and acceptance from a man.

My faith had been deeply shaken. I was a strange child, by all accounts, preferring to spend my time with adults and holding interest in topics most eight-to-eleven-year-olds barely know exist. I was fascinated by my religion and soaked up every sermon and every Bible verse I could. My grandmother had bought me a bible, that I still have on my bookshelf, and together we carefully attached golden-tipped plastic labels for easier referencing.

In her upbringing, and under her brother's teachings as the pastor of our church, it was common to highlight passages and make notes in them along the way during sermons. Her brother would cite the page number and verse, and everyone would dutifully shuffle their bibles in unison. His style of preaching involved frequent and rapid jumping from one section of the Bible to the next, so you had to be paying attention. The tabs helped.

My grandmother had gotten into the habit years prior to using a highlighter to mark every verse he referenced. She proudly demonstrated her years-long dedication, flipping through brightly colored pages with dozens of rainbow bars, sometimes entire pages full. She joked that she was curious if he would eventually reference every verse in the Bible.

My bible was similar, but not as full of color just yet. Sitting next to her, I would carefully mark each passage, feeling a sense of satisfaction. She also wrote notes and thoughts along the edges with arrows pointing to their respective verse. I did the same.

I believed that the answers to my life were in that book somewhere and I had to piece together the puzzle to figure it out. My life had to have a purpose. I couldn't just exist to move from one torment to the next without any understanding of why. As a Christian, pain and suffering are within the context of expected experience. But I had to know more.

As I got older, my search settled in on the very last book of the Bible, *Revelation*, which details the end of the world. The symbolism, which in my church was understood to be quite literal representations of the future, filled my imagination. I would escape into Biblical fantasy, laying in the grass, staring up at the sky, and going over the timeline in my head.

At one point I had a highly disturbing and vivid dream where I woke up to realize the Rapture was happening and I ran outside to see the souls of the saved rising into the air all around me. In a moment of pure panic, I desperately called out to Jesus who appeared before me and calmly told me my role was to stay behind and help those doomed to suffer through the Tribulation period of global destruction.

I woke up deeply troubled but resigned to my fate and every day after found myself contemplating the revelation I would not be joining my grandmother and the others at my church when the Rapture came. I believed it was my calling to suffer with the damned but knowing I could save a few and play a part in God's plan relieved some of that anxiety.

Naturally this was uncomfortable for adults to hear an eight- or nine-year-old discuss with determination and despair. My grandmother considered it to be God speaking to me in a dream and that it must be true. The Bible apparently spoke of such individuals being chosen and she felt I should be proud to be one of them. Everything in my life seemed to point to the same truth, I was meant to suffer. At least, it seemed, that suffering had a purpose.

I always carried that knowledge in the back of my mine, especially during discussions at church of this particular subject. While the pastor would talk about the terrifying events of this period in future history and wax poetic on the glorious salvation of the true believers, I would turn my eyes downward, feeling a sense of loss and separation.

The sudden realization that I was somehow inherently something that God referred to as an abomination was nearly too much for my young psyche to handle. Every time I would approach the front of the church during the latter part of the service when the pastor urged those unsaved to commit to the faith, I found the experience empty and hollow.

I just couldn't feel whatever it was everyone else was feeling, no matter how much I concentrated, repeated the phrases, or begged. Perhaps I was never meant to be saved, I thought. Perhaps I was simply unsavable.

This conflict haunted me into my teenage years when I desperately searched for some spiritual answer that seemed intentionally kept away from me. I had convinced myself, though, that my nature and my actions with the man I trusted kept me from God.

In my teenage years I sought a religious solution to my homosexuality, exploring what my pastor called "reparative" therapy. We would meet once a week and talk through my thoughts and urges and he would instruct me to fight them with everything I had. I had no attraction to women at all, but he assured that would come in time.

As I got older, my ability to suppress my sexual feelings became more difficult and far more frustrating. It seemed like an endless struggle I couldn't win. Once again, the thought that perhaps if I were a girl, none of this would be a barrier to happiness was compelling.

I had as much control over my emotions and thoughts as I did my spiritual fate. No level of intention impacted the outcome, and I relied on the mercy of others. Everything in my world told me I was broken, that I was wrong. The struggle to find control seemed to only produce the outcome that I had none.

Shortly after I moved to Florida, my new parents took me to a Christian bookstore where I discovered an entire world of study existed. Overwhelmed with the vast array of choices, I frantically sifted through books trying to make a selection before my parents were ready to leave. My mom collected Precious Moments figurines and had decided to make an impulsive stop in the store.

My stepfather, who didn't particularly share the same enthusiasm towards religion in general, was unhappy with encouraging what he saw as an unhealthy obsession on my part. My mother, however, wanted to encourage my interests and decided it couldn't hurt.

I settled on an intriguing novel set during the Tribulation. I began reading it before we walked out of the store, and I would read it over and over again. The story follows a young girl in her early teens witnessing the Rapture take place and realizing her bored attitude at church had betrayed her. It follows a parallel story of a young man in his early twenties do the same, but with contrasting outcomes.

The teenage girl, suddenly without her family and on her own, survives the events of Revelation, page by page, until she is imprisoned for her faith and given the choice to either take the mark of the Beast or be burned alive as a martyr. The young man faces the same choice.

She chooses to be a martyr and he chooses to take the mark, damning his soul but experiencing a temporary sense of freedom and purpose as he eventually helps to persecute Christians. The final two scenes have stuck with me ever since, one an image of the teenage girl tied to a stake and burned alive as she sings praises to God, not feeling the pain, and one of the damned young man pleading for rocks to crush him as he sees Jesus arrive with his army of angels.

Although I would not recommend such graphic stories to an eleven-year-old today, at the time it was a remarkable experience for me seeing the future I believed I would live through. As a believer left behind to suffer through the Tribulation, my fate would inevitably face that same decision. I could be persecuted, ultimately being martyred like the young girl or betray my faith and be damned.

It was strangely comforting, and I identified with the young woman intensely. I would go on to be known as "church boy" at my new school, where I carried the book with me, and my bible. At church, our pastor believed that the Rapture would happen soon as there had to be a seven-year gap between it and the end of the world, which he believed was the year 2000, which meant it had to happen that year.

I was ready and accepted I would never have a wife or children; I would never become a pastor of my own church like my grandmother wanted and I wouldn't even go to college. Without a future to worry about, I found a temporary sense of relief and purpose.

When I returned to live with my father, my search for a place in my faith became even harder because he was deeply antagonistic towards religious people. Even though he had tried to gain the approval of his uncle and his mother by attending a local Christian college, with the intent to become ordained, he gave up shortly after. My grandfather agreed with him.

I walked to multiple churches in my area, but I felt out of place. I would sit and listen, try to feel what they felt, try to fit in and join along, but it felt forced. As I got older, I would feel intense guilt and paranoia that everyone there knew I was gay and would reject me the moment they found out.

I would eventually recover a moment of that peace when a new friend I met at work invited me to his church and, having a crush on him, I agreed. Although I was skeptical, I sat with his wife as he gave a guest sermon that Sunday. He was studying to become a pastor.

As he told his own story of recovering from drug addiction and finding his own faith, I felt moved. My crush transformed into admiration and respect and witnessing the collective release themselves from their lives and join together spiritually, I felt contentment.

After the service I thanked him for inviting me and there was a part of me that felt whole again. I didn't find any new answers, but I did find good people who knew I was gay and welcomed me any way. So much of my fear, insecurity and resentment evaporated that morning and I walked away grateful for the experience.

SIX

Twink

Shortly before my fourteenth birthday I traveled back to Ohio for a mandatory visit with my father over the Summer. He had divorced his wife and convinced the court he could provide a safe place for me, and the courts agreed. It was the realization I needed to care for my grandfather that kept me there.

My dad was different, older, calmer. Since both his and my grandfather's divorce, the two had reconnected and become close. They had overcome their history in which my grandfather's drinking created a massive rift with his son. My dad, who had long despised his father, found him to be the last comfort in his world after everything else was taken from him. The new hope of having both his children with him again inspired him.

But I was never the same. Something in me broke the moment he pulled from me that day on the courthouse steps. I had reached out to comfort him, as I had so many times before, and his cold rejection created a wall I could not find a reason to let down. I was nearly fourteen, but I felt as though I had the weight of many lifetimes on my shoulders. The realization of what I had done sexually, and the profound sense of spiritual loss and abandonment had become all-consuming. Yet I couldn't talk about any of it.

I spent that summer quietly contemplating my future sitting out on my grandfather's deck, staring at the river I found so much peace in as a child. That peace was gone. The house that was once my sole source of comfort and joy had become cold and empty. My grandfather had long lived upstairs while my grandmother downstairs. I didn't think anything of it as a child, but now the only warm place was upstairs, watching TV with my grandfather.

My grandmother had quickly moved on after divorcing my grandfather. After decades of marriage, she finally got up one morning and decided it was enough and she left. She didn't stay lonely for long though and she remarried the day the divorce was finalized. My grandfather would live in the house until he passed, and she would move on with her new husband.

Without her, the bedroom had become a tomb, with discarded remnants of her hurried collection of possessions years before. Her once brimming closet full of colorful treasures was left empty and disheveled during her desperate but determined escape. There were pieces of her everywhere, still in the spot she originally put them, but she was gone. I decided to move in with my grandfather to help fill that empty space.

My dad worked at a local college, and I spent a lot of time exploring its campus. When I was seven or eight years old my dad would bring me with him to work on occasion, usually during the summer. I got used to wandering the Science building, where he was the chemistry stockroom manager. The campus was built in 1837 and the original buildings were still in use. I loved exploring the ancient buildings, touching the walls, and imagining all the life that happened there.

One of my favorites was the library. It was a massive building with a dramatic entrance with grand high ceilings and gorgeous architecture. The areas added on to accommodate the growing student population were less impressive, built in the 1970's. These areas were known as "the stacks," and were both fascinating and intimidating for me.

Each floor of the stacks had access from an old elevator that frequently trapped people inside for hours at a time, and old, dark stairways. The entrance was tucked away in a corner and down a long narrow hallway horizontal floor to ceiling shelves were placed against one wall. It was notorious as a place for college students to engage in behavior outside of their academic studies for its inherent privacy.

This desirable quality was also dangerous. The long hallway was maybe four or five feet wide, just enough to push a book cart through, and each shelving unit was flat against the other wall, creating a one-way entrance with no escape. If you needed a book at the far end of the shelf, you were essentially trapped.

The old florescent lights flickered endlessly and created a dark yellow glow that absorbed into the dark red brick walls and dingy yellow, orange, and tan floor tiles. Off to one side was a larger room with a few tables in the center and lined with more bookcases. It too had only one entrance in. There were no library employees stationed in these areas.

Nevertheless, I found the enclosed, dimly lit hallways hauntingly comforting. Legends of ghosts wandering the stacks, stories my father loved to try and frighten me with, only increased my curiosity and I would sometimes sit on the floor against the wall as silently as I possible, and just wait and listen, hoping to catch a glimpse of those lost souls.

At fourteen, having just reunited with my Ohio family, the library provided a sense of isolated security and familiarity. I would ask my grandfather or father to drop me off in front of the massive, opulent front entrance where I journeyed up the long walkway towards huge wooden doors. I would disappear behind them, and my dad or grandfather assumed I was perfectly safe.

When I was ready to be picked up, I used a payphone just outside one of the campus-facing entrances.

I was alone in this library one evening, exploring the expansive basement, which felt more like a maze, looking for the perfect book to entertain myself with and as I browsed an older man noticed me and began following me. I became aware of him but assumed I was safe in a public place, and I simply was not prepared for when he approached me and grabbed my crotch in the restroom.

I was fascinated by the sexual graffiti on the walls inside the stalls of the bathrooms at the college, curiously reading the messages, a proto-chat room, following the stories left there. Men would write back and forth to each other, scheduling meetings with locations and other men would comment back.

I didn't fully understand that it was all sexual, but it certainly felt forbidden. I got into the habit of exploring all the men's restrooms I could find so I could sneak in and browse the often-explicit conversations written on the walls. That evening I had used the bathroom, was alone and decided to check out the stalls.

It was the stall furthest to the wall, meant for handicap access, which contained the bulk of the messages. It also had a medium sized hole cut out between the dividing wall of the stall next to it. I was too busy investigating the rudimentary drawings and sexually explicit messages to notice that another person had entered the restroom.

When I heard the door loudly slam shut, I instantly felt exposed in my exploration and I instinctively jumped out of the stall, quickly composing myself and walking to the sink to wash my hands. The older man, short and round with balding grey hair, walked directly to the sink and washed his hands as well, looking at me with an intense and intrusive stare.

Uncomfortable, I quickly moved past him and back into the open room, choosing one of the hallways and disappearing. I waited for the door to slam shut again and then peaked around the corner to see if he had left. I then returned to the bathroom to continue examining the walls in the stall. He had also not gone far and upon hearing the door slam, returned as well.

This time when I jumped out of the stall, he stood facing me, blocking my exit. I tried to move past him but without breaking his stare, he stopped me with one hand and with the other he grabbed my crotch. My eyes widened as I had assumed I was going to get in trouble for reading the pornographic material.

Without removing his firm grip on my crotch, he led me out into the open hallway and into the larger public area where he positioned me atop the steps and proceeded to unzip my pants and drop to his knees. My reaction, as I remember, was somewhere between utter shock and dizzying fear as I imagined I would get in trouble if I made noise or pulled away. I remember believing as an adult he had authority over me, and I was instantly transported back to that mental place the man I trusted had taken me.

My body responded instinctively, but my mind was static. He engaged in sexual activity as I stood frozen, confused, and afraid of anyone walking by. Forcing me to have an orgasm, standing in an open space, with a few steps down to a public sitting area, was both exhilarating and terrifying. I felt completely out of control, unable to move and held hostage by my conflicting physical and mental emotions. The man, pleased with himself, patted me on the shoulder and walked away, leaving me standing with my pants still unzipped, stunned by what just happened.

I stayed there, shaken, for some time, unable to focus my mind and waiting for, what I assumed, the police to arrive and arrest me. My paralysis was compounded by my fear, and I lost time, finding myself standing outside holding a phone to my ear and asking my dad to pick me up. I don't even remember how I got the words out; it was purely automatic.

I remember waiting for my dad to take me home in a daze, convinced he must have known and preparing for punishment. But he didn't know, and I simply rationalized it and moved on. But it also made me curious about why a stranger would do that to me and what it meant that I enjoyed the experience.

I went back to the library again a few days later, I lost the days in between, and I ventured back down to the basement out of an almost instinctual curiosity. I stood facing the place where the older man had assaulted me, looking the ghost of myself in the eyes as I imagined my previous self looking back at me and pleading for help. I must have stood there in a trance for quite a while, only broken from it by the unexpected movement of another person nearby.

I caught a glimpse of the person, a student, dashing from one area to another as I carefully followed his shadow. He moved into one of the stacks and I chose one a few rows back, intensely staring through the gaps. I caught his glance, he held it for a moment and then disappeared again, only to shuffle into a closer row.

Grabbing a random book, I opened it and held my breath as I heard him shuffle again. This time, though, he had moved into my row. I was closer to the wall, trapped, and he was pretending to browse the books, glancing over to me. He was astonishingly attractive, and I couldn't look away.

This was apparently a signal to him that I was interested and despite his being a bit shorter than me, I hit my adult height at 6'1 that year, he confidently approached me, put his hand on my shoulder, repositioned me and then reached up a kissed me.

His kiss was passionate, and I felt a sense of being overwhelmed that I did not know was possible. He guided me through various sexual activities, and I remember how absolutely enthralled I was with his every touch and look. Seemingly lost in his own fantasy adventure, he wanted responded to every hint of another person's presence by grabbing my hand and hurrying down another hallway.

At one moment in our spontaneous romance, he pulled me into a darkened corner where someone had decided to place a few large wooden bookshelves on a raised area with only two, maybe three feet space from the wall. There he pushed my back against the brick wall and passionately made out with me. I was living a scene I had only witnessed in movies. I had stumbled by pure accident onto a secret location where I soon came to realize, boys like me were valued.

Afterwards he didn't scurry away like the other man did, and his aggressive passion had exhausted my young brain in a way I couldn't predict. He babbled on about his life and his interests and I stared back, silently, intensely focused but unable to understand anything happening to me.

Grabbing my hand, he pulled me towards the elevator and once safely inside, latched back onto me with another round of passionate kissing before abruptly composing himself just as the doors opened. Walking out into the large and crowded main level, he quickly let go of my hand, shoved his own into his pockets, and looked around suspiciously, nodding for me to follow him.

I carefully followed, confused and paranoid that every other person in the room was watching us and knew what we just did. We entered a small computer lab, recently installed with a few long tables and a half dozen monitors available for use. Logging in, he whispered to me questions about my knowledge of the internet and email. Confirming I had no idea what he was talking about, he quickly navigated to Hotmail to set up an account for me.

Smiling at me, scanning me up and down, he discreetly squeezed my leg under the table and typed in "Boxerbriefboy" and a random number I don't remember, creating my very first email account. My password was my birthdate. He then signed out, logged into his own account, and sent me a quick message. He had to leave, but he wanted to meet again. With another round of careful assessment of his surroundings, he winked at me and scurried away out the door. I just sat there, motionless.

That night on my way home I was dreamy. I couldn't stop thinking about him, about what we did and how passionate and affectionate he was. It was close to Christmas as I lounged on the couch, staring at the lights bouncing off the walls and I became lost in a fantasy. Had I just met my soulmate? Was this love? It was all happening so fast.

The next evening, I begged my dad to take me back to the library. He finally agreed, annoyed he had to get dressed for the cold just to drive me there. I assumed my new boyfriend would be there waiting for me. I ran up the walkway, completely oblivious to my dad or anyone else nearby seeing me and I immediately darted down the stairs to the basement.

There I waited, ears on hyperalert, holding in my breath every time I heard the ding of the elevator or what I thought sounded like footsteps. In the stacks it was common to hear footsteps without encountering another person. I went back to my row where he found me, and I paced impatiently. I didn't have a computer and I couldn't log onto the one upstairs because I wasn't a student. I didn't really understand what email was anyway.

He didn't show up that night. After hours of frustrated waiting, I finally gave up, imagining the worst and shuffling out into the long hallway. I had to use the bathroom and so I made my way to the men's room which faced the entrance of the stairs, had a seating area and a few broken vending machines.

Entering the bathroom again, a tall man was using one of the four available urinals. I took the second to the left, providing an empty urinal between us. Crestfallen, I paid no attention to the other man and just looked down. Out of the corner of my eye, however, I noticed movement and when I glanced over, he was looking directly at me, masturbating.

I found that once a man touched me and began guiding me, I was helpless, even if I didn't want to do anything with him in particular. There were times I felt disgusted and yet I never backed away or said no. The occasions when I enjoyed myself, I imagined I had made a friend who cared about me because why else would a man kiss me, touch me in such a way and be so intimate with me?

I continued returning to the same location over and over hoping to find that young man again, but without fail, would find myself pulled away by a different man each time. Most were gentle and affectionate. I was never shy about my age, and it didn't seem to matter.

In my late twenties I stumbled upon one of the men online who remembered me from that time, and he told me that what made me stand out was my youth and my eagerness to please. He and the other men, who knew each other, frequently talked about me and frequently told others of the tall, skinny young teenager that was reliably found in the library basement stacks.

For weeks I continued this remarkably dangerous journey with my parents often a floor or two above me never knowing and I felt so grown up and attractive. Everyone told me how beautiful I was, how sexy and how perfect. I thought this is what being an adult was like. I thought that after everything, this was simply my place, just as the man I trusted told me.

But the magical thinking never lasted beyond the boundaries of that particular place and time, and I would find myself lying in bed with thoughts racing of what it meant for me to have had so many sexual partners in secret. I had prided myself on my vow to wait until marriage to have sex. Once that vow was broken, I believed I was damaged and unlovable. The encounters I continued having in this place temporarily felt like validation but were always frustratingly fleeting.

I went to school and felt out-of-place among my peers who, if they were having sex were engaging with each other and usually within some form of a relationship. I couldn't talk to anyone and often the anxiety, fear and paranoia reached such a high pitch in my mind I could not focus at all. Yet the compulsion to continue exploring, searching, and hoping that one of these men would actually love me back kept me returning to that basement bathroom.

The compulsion never left me and throughout my teen years I engaged in astonishingly reckless behavior in my attempts to both satisfy my sexual urges and my deep desire for love and acceptance from a man.

Throughout, my isolation from my family became profound as I developed an awareness of how destructive the behavior truly was. Why didn't my father ever know? My stepmother even once shouted into the open elevator for me because she was impatient waiting and the man who was engaged with me at the time responded with a flabbergasted, "really" when I told him it was my mom.

I experienced even more profound depression and anxiety as I merely attended school but could not feel connected to any of my classmates. Even before I officially came out, I would often gaze across the room at these young relatively innocent lives worried about homework, sports and excitedly hoping their parents would be gone for just long enough to make out with their boyfriend or girlfriend and I felt completely alone. I'd have had more sexual partners before I turned sixteen than would all of my classmates combined in their entire lives.

Alone with my grandfather, I was largely on my own and I had recently been introduced to the internet. As the internet evolved, so did my sexual experiences and I went so far as to meet men I only chatted with for a few moments online with absolutely nothing to go on but their brief self-description and instructions to wait in a nearby parking lot for their car to arrive. At fifteen I was standing outside, alone, in empty parking lots at 1AM waiting for complete strangers to pick me up for sex in their cars.

The contrast between my life at school, going to the mall with my grandfather, watching TV while eating dinner and keeping up with my homework and my secret life at night was unsustainable. The pull of the remaining innocence of this time period against the pull of a world that seemed full of possibilities and pleasures was too much for me.

I wanted to be a kid. I became obsessed with *Nickelodeon*, cartoons, and stuffed animals. I wanted to have friends and do well in school and I wanted that connection to my church and to Andy and to something larger than myself again. But night after night, alone in an empty house with only the muffled sound of my grandfather's TV upstairs in the distance, I felt compelled to take on an adult life I believed was my only chance for happiness.

To make matters worse, I was still dedicated to finding that young college student but could not remember the password he set up for me. Nothing I tried worked. I believed if I could just find him again, I wouldn't have to search any longer and he and I could finally be together. He and I were never again at the library at the same time, if he had gone back at all, and I felt more and more desperate and hopeless trying to find him.

I would eventually though, as I recognized his face in a chat when I was on my own in my mid-twenties'. It was really him, but he had changed so much since I saw him last. He had dark features with large bright blue eyes and a slim muscular build when I first met him. Now his face looked worn and was covered with the obvious wounds of meth addiction.

He remembered me too, but not in the same way as I had. He saw me as a cute kid he got to have fun with and that was it. It seems he was arrested on drug charges shortly after he left the library that evening and was later charged with sexually abusing other minors. He had been in jail nearly the entire time I had spent looking for him and fantasizing about our future together.

One evening, my grandfather was cutting carrots for dinner when he suddenly paused and called my name. I was at the computer in the next room and when I turned, he had sat down. He was staring with a look of terror and was shaking. My stomach immediately fell, and I ran to the phone and called 911 as I watched him slump over. As he was taken away on a stretcher out the door, I saw his face and it was partially paralyzed, while the other half was frightened. I'd never seen my grandfather frightened before.

He had suffered a stroke and when he returned home, he was largely unable to function on his own. Despite this, at sixteen, I was left responsible for him, and I genuinely had no idea what to do. I began caring for myself entirely as he lived upstairs, unable to venture down any longer. I never quite understood the full gravity of the situation, and being a teenager, essentially living on my own, I lost all perspective on what a normal life was supposed to be.

The last remaining rituals of my innocence instantly evaporated. My grandfather would occupy much of my time with activities like cooking, gardening, going to the store or the mall and generally being active with him. I would sit on the couch with him and watch TV, exploring his coin collection and talking about my day, just as I did when I was a child. He would drive me to school and reliably be waiting in his car to pick me up after. We would drive to a fast-food place on the way home.

All of that was gone now as he laid on his couch, a shell of who he was before, staring blindly at the TV. I would frequently venture upstairs to see him sitting, motionless, gazing mindlessly at static, the blinking movement of the black, grey, and white noise highlighting the dark room with random and unsettling shadows.

I found myself avoiding him as much as possible, refusing to accept his disability and stubbornly holding onto the hope he would get better. This hope fell apart, though, when one evening he weakly called out for me, asking me to make him a sandwich and I realized he hadn't been eating on his own.

As my sexual encounters increased, I withdrew even further, and my grandfather's awareness dissipated in parallel. He soon forgot who I was, referring to me as my father. My father and aunt largely avoided the house, or any contact with him, except for my father helping himself to my grandfather's small pension and savings.

By my senior year in high school, I was dangerously close to failing and even closer to dropping out, and no one noticed. I was entirely responsible for getting myself to and from school, and since I couldn't drive, I just walked. It became easier and easier to not get up in the morning at all.

The house began to fall apart, and I started to invite men over for easy convenience. A string of adult men would come to the house and have sex with me while my grandfather was oblivious upstairs. I was able to separate the experience in my mind, disassociating and adopting and adult perspective during, only to revert to a scared and ashamed teenager after.

My grandfather, before he forgot me, feared I would turn out like his younger brother had. I went over to my stepmother's house, the only property my dad ever owned after winning a settlement from a car crash only to sign it away to her simply to get her out of his life, to attend a party my younger sister was having. When I returned, my grandfather sternly lectured me on the dangers of spending time with boys a few years younger than me.

My dad seemed entirely unaware and only my grandmother, who had recently moved back into the house next door, noticed my comings and goings, quizzing me on occasion to my profound embarrassment. My aunt, who would call to talk to my grandfather, knew and after I came out, was the first to tell me no one was surprised.

Yet no adult in my life knew that I was up until the early hours of the night in adult gay chat rooms, making phone calls to men all over the country for phone sex, or rushing out the door to meeting strangers for sex in their car. Looking back at how close I came to true danger, it astonishes me. I once rode my bike after midnight several miles away into another state to meet a man parked in a dark lot facing the river front, known for shootings and drug activity. After out encounter in his car, I rode my bike back and spent the next several days attempting to hide the choke marks on my neck.

No one noticed.

My struggle to accept my sexuality had consumed me to the point that the very notion of gender had been suppressed. I associated my femininity with being gay and every sexual encounter tended to involve me being submissive and feminine. In the gay male world, this is known as a "twink." A boyish, skinny, feminine man who looks like a teenager. Of course, I was a teenager and that was the appeal for so many men I engaged with.

Just as the man I trusted years before had promised, my ticket into being accepted by other men was through sexually pleasuring them. That acceptance was fleeting, and I rarely encountered the same man twice. The longer it went on, the more ashamed I felt and the less I imagined my worth would be. Soon it became mechanical, something to satisfy the urges and achieve momentary bliss in the rare, but profound affection from men who chose moments of kindness.

During that year, one man did hang around, however. Rather than meeting through the internet or at the library, friends I had made through theater introduced me to him. He was a bit older, in his early twenties, and I found him absolutely breathtaking. He was mostly unimpressed with me but seemed to enjoy spending a few hours a week with me showering him with adoration.

He was overly aggressive, however, to the point of being abusive. I still have a scar under my collar bone from him pushing a sharpened fingernail into my skin. He only responded to me positively when I submitted to his violent and painful sexual demands, and then largely dismissed or ignored me afterwards. I was desperate, confused and believed him when he told me that I was damaged goods.

The different experience with him though, was that he overtly treated me as a girl. He frequently encouraged me to behave as feminine as possible, even situating my genitals to resemble those of a woman. He referred to me as his girlfriend and often explained in great detail how my role was to essentially be a better kind of girl, for his enjoyment. Rather than be offended or discouraged, this seemed to finally make sense to me.

He soon grew bored of me and simply left one day and never answered his phone again, but for me his impact was long-lasting. I had proven how much pain I could take and how dedicated I was to him, but in the end that didn't matter. What mattered was how I made him feel, and being more like a girl made him happier, and often less violent.

I realized that once again, after years of suppression, that I could never be masculine enough to earn the acceptance of men, but maybe I could be feminine enough to. I began to inundate myself with gay media, films, books, and magazines. Gay men were mostly feminine stereotypes, but they often earned the attention of masculine men around them. I decided gay media was my ticket out of isolated, parking lot shame and into the real world of men who would appreciate me.

Before my grandfather was disabled, he and I took weekly trips to the mall, where since I was seven, had been a Friday evening ritual. As a child my grandparents and I would eat at the same restaurant by the movie theater, and then venture out to the same stores. I had an allowance and would dedicate my five dollars a week to buying four items at the dollar store. It was one of the few things that tied me to the innocent and joyful parts of being a child.

During these trips, my grandmother would usually head to the shoe outlets and my grandfather would find a nice place on a bench to relax and watch the other shoppers hurry along their way. I would usually go with my grandmother, and I loved spending an hour or longer with her as she tried on dozens of shoes, examined new dresses, purses and scarves and tried on new accessories.

When I returned from my mother's, my grandfather once again started up the tradition, getting himself out of the house. On one trip he found his bench and I ran off to the small bookstore nearby to indulge my interest in books. I bought a new one almost every week. The bookstore had a tiny gay and lesbian section with maybe 10 or less books that rarely changed. I had come to know them all by heart.

One in particular, a humor book called, *The Homo Handbook*, by Judy Carter, stood out to me and it piqued my curiosity. With a great deal of internal dialogue and practice, I finally got the nerve to take the book to the counter to buy it. The cashier barely raised an eyebrow, but I was too busy looking for my grandfather to notice if he did.

In the plastic bag, the cover could just barely be seen, and so I bought a random magazine to try and disguise it. I had to get the book past my grandfather, get it home and hide it before he noticed. It was absolutely terrifying. I felt like I had committed a crime.

I succeeded however and, in my grandmother's once bursting walk-in closet, I hid behind a pile of old clothes and carefully tiptoed into the book's contents. By that evening I was staring in the mirror, following one recommended exercises in the book, and saying the words, "I am a homosexual."

That moment changed my future and opened up a new world of identity, purpose and hope for belonging. I quickly purchased several of the other books, and after my grandfather could no longer drive, rode my bike to the bus station to take myself to the bookstore.

I bought magazines as well. Magazines were much less discreet and buying them made me feel bold and I began testing out the idea that I could be gay in public. The cashier was never impressed, as far as I could tell. Each new book and magazine strengthened my sense of identity and belonging, and I felt as though I was studying for my eventual escape into the gay world. A place I fervently believed was my true home.

There was also a small video rental store within walking distance I frequented, which carried several gay and lesbian titles, and I rented the movie, *The Object of My Affection*, starring Paul Rudd and Jennifer Aniston, so many times the owner offered to give it to me for free.

At home, alone with a whole house to myself, I spent hours and hours looking into these windows of a happier future where I might finally be free to be myself and be accepted. As my identity as a gay man strengthened, my attitude towards my sexual activities changed as well.

I began to see it as part of my identity, and part of being a proud and confident gay man. In the comedy *Jeffrey*, starring Patrick Stewart and Steven Weber, the main character makes a joke with a new love interest that he would be willing to provide the special and exclusive physical connection he had only shared with 5,000 other men. My promiscuity was shameful in the straight world, but a sign of pride in the gay one.

The movies, magazines, online resources, chatrooms and so on, all indicated that being gay meant being free from the restrictions of heterosexual society and that meant freedom to explore sex as much as one pleased. I embraced this philosophy fully and safe in my private kingdom, I let go of every inhibition surrounding gender and sexuality I had. I wrapped myself in flowing silk fabric I found at a local fabric store and danced around the room I once occupied with my grandmother watching Christian programs on the degradation of morals in our culture.

Gender seemed to be meaningless in this world as gay men in gay media openly defied all concepts of masculinity while chasing after straight men who embodied it. It was a festival of individuality and expression and I wanted to be a part of it. By my senior year in high school, all I cared about was escaping to California and joining my people and never looking back. I reasoned I would be valued for my sexual skills and that would open the door to gay society and allow me to fully integrate. I practiced being a gay person with determination.

Despite the conflict between the real-life experiences of meeting men online for sex, or talking with them on the phone sexually, or spending hours chatting with them, discussing, again, sex, it all felt worth it if I could join the rainbow-painted world of San Francisco or New York.

I covered my belongings with rainbow stickers and symbols boldly declaring same-sex love. I often sashayed my way down the hallways at school, when the mood hit me, soaking up the attention from my fellow classmates who had no idea what to think.

But it was lonely, still. At the end of the day, it was performance art for no one in particular and the only person who even knew what it meant was me. Alone in my grandfather's house, draped in flowing fabric and carefully mimicking the most flamboyant drag queens and gay men I could find in movies, I was still just acting. It was all simply another costume I hoped would win me approval and acceptance, from society, and maybe if I was lucky, another man.

SEVEN

Could I Really Be a Girl?

My grandfather passed away two days before my eighteenth birthday. I awoke on a Saturday morning to a bright and cheery sun cascading through the upstairs window. A few weeks before, after another trip to the emergency room, my grandfather was assigned an aid to help him with his daily tasks. He moved downstairs and began to improve. We were even sitting and watching TV together again and his lapses in memory were less frequent.

But that morning it was unusually quiet and as I descended the stairs, I saw him slumped over on the floor. He had died earlier that morning. His funeral was on my birthday, and I entered adulthood feeling a sense of devastation I had not been prepared for. Concerned for his potentially valuable coin collection and paranoia of my potential reaction, I was locked out of the house that evening. Several hours later, after midnight, I was sleeping at a friend's house when my father arrived and told me my grandfather's house, my only safe place in the world, was on fire.

I arrived to see it completely engulfed in flames. Before my eyes everything I knew and loved vanished in smoke. Authorities believed it was set by either my father or his uncle, my grandfather's youngest brother, who set it out of spite. According to my grandparent's divorce agreement, my grandmother was the owner of the property, and my grandfather was living in it at no cost. Once he passed, she would get the house and property. She and her husband had moved into the house next door, the one I grew up in.

A year prior my sister moved back in with our mother in Florida and so the house he rented was occupied by him and my little brother on weekends. I moved in with nothing from my previous life and found myself remarkably unprepared for adulthood. I got my first job that year and my driver's license. I began to engage more socially, bonding with friends I had met very recently. For the first time in my life, I had gay friends and straight friends who happily accepted my gayness.

My sexual life was still very secretive. As adulthood removed all limitations from my seemingly endless exploration of available men in the area, my encounters increased in both frequency and recklessness. But I also found myself in a state of identity flux. I had accepted my Christian faith had abandoned me and so I aggressively began searching for a replacement.

Some of my new friends were Wiccans, and so I became one too. I tried on new identities as frequently as I could dye my hair and change my outfits and I experienced a sort of delayed adolescence. I was suddenly inundated with a social life I never experienced before and the childhood I equally never indulged came bursting out.

About this time, the realization of practical transgender transition came into my view. It happened quite by accident while watching TV and happening upon a documentary that followed a man as he went through transition. He had been in the military, had desperately tried to fit in as a man and finally decided he would be happier as a woman. A lightbulb came on.

Could I really become a woman? What would that mean for me if I did? I suddenly became overwhelmed with the dysphoria that plagued my childhood and my head began spinning with the possibilities. With equal parts elated hope and overwhelming despair at the impossibility of it all, I became obsessed with the process and the realities involved.

The first step was talking with a therapist. You know how I feel about therapists. I was still under my father's insurance, so I was able to find someone fairly easily. The conversation, however, did not go as expected. My therapist was a woman I had seen in high school after I had been outed to my father and half the faculty. When I was sixteen, a teacher heard that I had recently talked about being gay with my friends and alerted the principal who alerted my father.

I found myself being called into a conference room with multiple school officials, a police officer, and my father, where the principal announced to the room that I had recently been telling people I was a homosexual. I had also displayed radical personality changes, memory loss, unpredictable behavior, and anti-social behavior they worried might become violent. This was the shortly after the Columbine school shooting in 1999.

As a result, I was taken out of school for a week and required to see a therapist. She was happy to see me back but concerned about the newest development I was bringing to her attention. She and I had long talks about what exactly it meant for me to live as a woman, size eleven shoes and baritone voice and all. I hit 6'1 by age fourteen, and despite being extremely skinny with slight features, I still looked very much like a man. She didn't imagine I would transition well.

The conversation was far less about how I felt and more focused on the practical matters. How would I pay for all the surgery and medical treatment required? How would I manage the social changes in a conservative area where I had spent most of my life? Could I accept being viewed as a man who became a woman and likely be rejected by straight men? She reasoned I was a gay man and therefore confusing my emotions with certainty that I must be a woman.

I disagreed with her, strongly, and found her persistent inquiry into the underlying factors involved frustrating. However, my gay friends agreed with her caution and so did two transgender women they introduced me to. Although my newfound identity made a lot of sense to most people who knew me, there was some disagreement on my ability to effectively pull it off. Through a series of friends, two older transgender women were brought in to evaluate the situation.

I will never forget how one reasoned it would be much better to be a feminine gay man with intact organs than an unhappy woman regretting a permanent choice. One of them fell into the latter category, lamenting her struggle with adapting to a body that simply did not function the way she had hoped it would. In her late fifties, she had fought for years for approval to transition, lived as a woman for a time, began hormone treatment and saved up to pay for the full surgery.

Yet, she woke up in the same body she began with, except this one didn't change how she felt about herself. She told me she felt deeply betrayed. There were many factors involved. She didn't pass well, she began balding, her voice never quite fit, and the men she was interested in were not interested in her. She suffered severe depression and attempted suicide several times.

Her friend had a much better personal experience, transitioning much more easily and passing well. She barely faced any difficulties in normal life, and she had a loving husband. But, she explained, it just isn't right for everyone. Forcing transition would do no more to alleviate my sense of not belonging, in my body or otherwise. It would likely only make things worse.

I was undeterred, however, determined that my dream man and my dream life required me to take this drastic step. I just had to find a way to get there. Although I couldn't necessarily see my immediate future, I did happily imagine myself primping in the bathroom mirror just as I had watched my grandmother do all those years ago. Perhaps if I transitioned, I thought, my grandmother would eagerly support me and leave me her jewelry. It seemed like the best plan I could come up with.

I still needed to find a therapist who would agree, another therapist who would agree with them and $50,000 for the entire experience. I worked part time at a pet store. Then there was the reality of living as a woman for a year or possibly two, before being approved for surgery. It seemed so unfair and contradictory. How was I supposed to get an idea of what living as a woman would be like if I was stuck as a man in a wig the whole time?

Obviously, my father would not approve, and I would have to see him every single day. Could I even keep working? I planned my rationale to my boss, explaining my choice and the consequences of it, but every time I approached her door, I became too nervous. I couldn't even get the nerve to shop in the women's section for clothing, let alone figure out what size I was and buy anything.

I decided to bring up the subject with my grandparents, perhaps becoming a woman would be more acceptable to them than living as a gay man. Interestingly, I wasn't too far off. When I carefully explained what I was experiencing, both my grandmother and her husband smiled broadly at each other and laughed to themselves. It all seemed to make sense to them all of a sudden.

My grandmother regaled me of stories of my childhood in which she seemingly beamed with joy watching me prance around as the granddaughter she always wanted. She admitted she'd secretly wished I was a girl, and she was disappointed she never had the opportunity to really bond with her other granddaughters. Her husband joked he knew it from the moment he asked me to hand him a tool while he was fixing his car and I picked it up as though it would bite me.

However, they were not as enthusiastic about the notion of paying for the procedure, very abruptly laughing at the notion. It wasn't so much out of dismissal or prejudice, but practicality. They didn't have that much money even if they wanted to. Besides, she reasoned, I was still young. There was plenty of time.

Feeling utterly defeated and finding no place to even begin, I sat that dream down on a shelf and decided until I could make any real decisions on the matter, now just wasn't the time. I felt sick at the thought of waiting years to begin my life, but I accepted I had no available options. The only thing I could do was wait.

It's interesting that it took me so long to figure out what transition was. The following summer after I returned to live with my father, I flew down to Florida for a short stay with my mother. One morning, we were mindlessly watching daytime TV and stumbled on a talk show about men who became women.

I remember my mom commenting that it was confusing to her since several of the 'before' pictures showed very attractive young men and the 'after' was far from an improvement. I remember squinting a bit, not understanding what I was looking at, but vaguely feeling like it was a costume or something. It just didn't click.

When I began diving into gay media, several movies included transgender characters, but they were played by obvious men, and I thought it was parody. Others seemed to tell stories of regret and hopelessness. Something that invoked pity, rather than inspiration.

One was featured in the comedy *Jeffrey*, where an obnoxiously dressed caricature of a New Jersey woman appeared in leopard print tights and a foot of burgundy curls on top her head, alongside her equally absurd mother. A famous scene involves Patrick Stewart, playing a flamboyant gay man, and the other main characters jumping into view of a clearly straight news reporter trying to do a live broadcast of a New York City gay pride parade.

The transgender character and his mother joined them and at a critical moment Stewart's character grabbed the mic and announced to the world that the transgender character would be having her penis removed the very next morning. "It's coming right off," her mother proclaimed.

In a more serious movie about a group of lesbian friends called, *Better Than Chocolate*, featured a storyline of a heterosexual man who transitioned into a woman and fell in love with one of the lesbian characters, who was adamantly uninterested.

The character's story came to an emotional peak when her parents bought her a new house. In a letter giving her the details, they explained, as she read aloud with tearful happiness, sliding slowly into devastating heartbreak, that the house was their last act as her parents, and they never wanted to see or speak to her again.

Beyond that, I had only adjacently been exposed to the physical realities of transition in niche porn featuring "shemales." The visual was an assault to my senses and certainly not a physical condition I wanted for myself.

The reality is, as a child I simply believed I could magically transform into a girl. I had no idea what that meant as I didn't know about female anatomy. All I knew was girls got to be pretty, wear cute clothes, have long hair and no one was chasing them around to go outside and play in the dirt.

I honestly didn't pay much attention to the physical development of girls around me as I was too preoccupied with my own. As obsessed as I was with women and dreaming of becoming one myself, I didn't really expect much to change about my actual body. I was more interested in the fashion.

The realities of being an actual female never crossed my mind. Hell, for quite an embarrassing amount of time I didn't even know girls pooped. My grandmother, to my knowledge, certainly did not. When she remodeled the house, adding on the large sitting room and upstairs space, she turned half of the master bedroom into her walk-in closet.

The downstairs bathroom was hidden at the end of a hallway, requiring passing through two separate doors and going past the walk-in closet. This was done on purpose, as she preferred her bathroom to be private and used only by her. My grandfather had a half-bath upstairs that was the primary use for he and I.

Whenever nature called, she would quietly excuse herself, disappear for a bit and then return without comment. I genuinely thought only boys used the bathroom and that was one of the key selling points to me for becoming a girl.

I never came up with a female name either. As many times as I renamed myself throughout my life, finding a female name that fit me was never intuitive and none of them sounded like, well, me. I notice many transgender people simply choose the opposite sex name of their own, but there is no female version of Chad.

As a child the thought never entered my mind. I wanted long hair. I wanted to wear makeup and pretty clothes. I wanted my own collection of beautiful jewelry and accessories. I wanted to prance around singing and dancing and I didn't want any of the responsibilities or obligations of being a boy.

Being a girl felt like the freest version of myself. Breasts felt more like an accessory to me. I didn't really have a preference or idea in mind, I just assumed they'd come with the package. Speaking of packages, I didn't really look down and contemplate much there either.

My body felt neutral to me. I thought it was all optional. Even as I began to seriously contemplate transition, I was focused mainly on the superficial qualities more than the practical ones. I didn't design my own vagina, as Laverne Cox's transgender character in *Orange is the New Black* boasted.

I was far more worried about my voice than I was what my future breasts would look like. When I fantasized about becoming a woman, it was always within the context of either fashion or attracting straight men. I wanted a TV movie romance with the man of my dreams while dressed in a stunning outfit and devastating hair.

My image of what a woman was entirely depended on stereotypes I stole from various role models over the years, and I never really developed my own sense of female personality. I assumed my female persona would be just like my current one, only in better clothes.

Looking back, I am astonished at how little thought I gave to actually living as a woman and what that would mean. It was more of a means to an end. My male body just wasn't working for me, and it was a relentless barrier to my personal expression and fantasies. I just needed a female body and all of that would resolve itself, I reasoned.

Womanhood was a costume to me, something I hoped to convincingly pull off and hide behind. It was superficial, artificial, and largely inconsequential. To me it didn't matter if I had a functional vagina and perfectly shaped breasts if my Adam's apple gave me away.

The further back into my memory I go, the less real women were to me. The world felt male and masculine. Women seemed like they were accessories within it. I watched my father treat women as playthings and heard him discuss them as such with his friends on more than one occasion.

My grandfather never stopped complaining of the annoyances of men and my grandmother seemed to live in a world she was forced to create on her, rather than one she fit into. Women were the outliers and men were the default. That is partially why I struggled so much. I couldn't manage to be the standard-issue boy that seemed to come so naturally to all the others.

My young mind reasoned that I could either become a superman or a woman, as my default setting wasn't good enough and it was causing me endless years of torment. But that wasn't really an understanding of either gender. It was simply the best way my adolescent mind could understand my own failure in socializing.

I can say that I didn't experience the often-cited phenomenon of feeling as though I was a literal female trapped in a male's body. For me it was a matter of practicality and given the choice, girls were just easier. I had no real concept of either sex beyond these superficial, observable, social interactions. To be honest, I have never encountered a transgender argument that leads me to believe anyone else has either.

As I entered my twenties, my priorities shifted, and I began to take the idea of college more seriously. I had given up on my education long ago, but after working multiple part time jobs that went nowhere and being constantly reminded by all my friends of how important and exciting college was, I decided to go for it. This my grandparents were happy to help fund.

My father announced a surprise marriage, to our surprise, and I moved out on my own for the first time. No longer living under the weight of my dad's depression and self-destructive behavior, I was able to consider my future, something I had given up on many times. I sat in my one-room apartment, and I contemplated my options. They seemed to be almost limitless.

Imagining living as a woman became a lot easier while on my own. I started by creating an artificial persona online, found photos from pornography sets and built an artificial life, engaging in what is now known as "catfishing." I wanted to see what it was like to talk to straight men as a woman.

The experience became intoxicating, however, and a simple experiment turned into an obsession. I would spend hours late at night talking to men in chatrooms, usually about sex, and feeling a strange sense of validation and satisfaction from the experience. I reasoned no one was getting hurt because they got a fantasy, and I got the emotional reward of seeing a side of men I had only imagined before.

Unlike gay men, sex chat with straight men was often more involved, more detailed, and frequently, more affectionate. Despite the temporary rush, it only deepened my feeling of hopelessness at ever finding anything meaningful in my life. With every response, I felt a heavy sense of dread and disappointment in the back of mind that I would never have any of it in real life.

I knew I could never be the women I was impersonating, but I also knew I could never find in gay men the qualities I desperately needed. My life was artificial no matter which direction I chose.

The next phase of exploration was, it seemed, drag. I had gone to gay bars infrequently, but the drag shows were always the most enjoyable part. However, I never looked to drag as effective female impersonation. The drag queens in my town, at least, were all obvious men who were portraying an exaggerated version of female stereotypes explicitly for humor. I doubt they could walk outside in the daylight and be mistaken for women.

But it seemed like a reasonable way to test out my chances of passing. I bought some Halloween makeup and a few wigs, and I borrowed a bra from a friend. As for clothes, I took a trip to my local Goodwill feeling confident no one would raise an eyebrow there. In the secret security of my apartment, I carefully lowered the blinds and attempted to piece together my new body with the resources I had collected.

To say it was an embarrassing failure would be a laughable understatement. I cannot even begin to describe how awkward and ridiculous I looked. I didn't laugh though, despite the absurdity staring back at me in the mirror. I just cried. How could I possibly live my life as a woman with the mess I was looking at? My body just did not work, my face didn't work, my voice didn't work. I couldn't be a man and it seemed, I couldn't be a woman, either.

I practiced being Britney Spears for a time, imagining her as my ideal female template. I wanted to perform her hit song, *Stronger*, at the gay bar. I felt a deep connection to that particular song and the dramatic change in character from her previous videos. It felt like the perfect platform for reinvention.

I took a chair and watched myself try my best to mimic her dance routine, over and over, deciding I would figure out the drag part later. It shocked me to discover that I was not a particularly good dancer, but I was confident in my ability to mimic her body language and facial expressions.

Despite my enthusiasm and dedication, at the end of the song I still saw my own reflection in the mirror, and I simply couldn't imagine my thin, rectangle body transforming into the curved devastating beauty that was Britney Spears.

Drag queens who are not naturally gifted with plump areas of their bodies to mold into effective illusions of female sensuality use padding. It would be many years until RuPaul taught me that on his show *RuPaul's Drag Race*. The work involved in taking a man's body and shaping it into a passable woman's body is involved.

Men must first "tuck" their privates. This requires popping the testicles up into the little sockets evolution provided as a safety precaution, and where they drop from during puberty. Once inside, they stay in place until they are 'popped' back out. It hurts.

The penis is then forced between the legs and taped down between the butt cheeks. This is also hurts. But it's the only way to ensure a smooth and flat bikini front. Depending on the desired look and the naturally available resources, padding is sculpted around the butt and thighs and then secured with layers of pantyhose.

Breasts are constructed by pushing the chest muscles together and securing them with a tight bra or top, if one is endowed with more fleshy mounds, they can easily resemble bouncing, natural breasts. Contouring with makeup provides a visual enhancement for the audience. A new trend involves wearing a large latex vest that secures over the shoulders to give a more convincing look of natural breasts.

Makeup requires multiple layers of heavy and dramatic shades of light and dark to pull the middle of the face forward and push the edges back, giving the face a glowing and pinched look, which is apparently more feminine.

Contouring around the jawline, brow and nose feminize the face and the eyes are given the illusion of being larger, deeper set and ringed with luscious, impossibly long, and full lashes. Tape is applied to the edges of the face just at the temples and pulled tightly back, elongating the eyes into a cat shape.

Makeup is then used to exaggerate the length and sharpness of the eye and brow. Natural eyebrows are forced flat using a glue stick and then artificial eyebrows are drawn above their natural placement, widening the eyes even further.

Blush is used to give the space just under the cheeks a deep and dark shadow with the apples dramatically highlighted to pop out. Many drag queens obtain plastic surgery specifically to enhance this part of the face, creating an unnaturally bulbous look when out of makeup.

The lips are exaggerated, with makeup surrounding the natural lines, to make them look as full as possible. To help this along, drag queens also use lip fillers and plumpers. The out-of-makeup effect is a fishlike face with perpetually pursed lips and massive cheekbones. To make things easier, professional drag queens usually shave their eyebrows, enhancing the alien look out of drag.

Finally, the wig is installed, which is exactly how they describe the procedure. First the natural hair is flattened, and a wig cap is put on, which is a very tight material, often repurposed pantyhose, which creates a perfectly smooth head. This is frequently secured into place with copious amounts of hairspray or gel.

The pre-styled wig is then placed on the head. Before lace front technology, a wig design in which several inches from the edge of the hair a sheer net is sewn in and hair strands are hand-tied into place to give the illusion of a visible scalp, queens had to melt the plastic strands at the edges to their face with a hairdryer. This was necessary to give the illusion of the hair growing out of the scalp rather than a sharp, unnatural line along the forehead and ears.

With lace technology in the front, sides and sometimes completely surrounding the head, the lace is cut short and then glued down. Glue is painted or sprayed onto the edges of the forehead, then the lace is pressed into place with more hairspray applied. Being transparent or nude colored, it blends in with the skin and additional makeup is used to hide any trace of it. Then the performer gets into their chosen outfit, puts on their jewelry and they're ready for the night.

There is a reason why my efforts to simply mimic the makeup of women I saw in regular life or in magazines did not provide me the feminized face I was hoping for, and those cheap wigs did me no favors either. The craft is in the illusion, which is unique for every face and takes years to master.

While many natural women do engage in such dramatic and frankly, unnecessary, lengths to disguise their flaws, most women do not require this level of effort to engage in day-to-day life. There is more to living as a woman than simply trying to look like one.

Transgender surgery often mirrors this reconstruction of the face. Beyond hormones, breast implants, and bottom surgery, transwomen frequently have facial surgeries as well. They will shave down their Adam's apple, shave the bone along their jawline and other areas of the face, and have silicone implants inserted in others.

The level of work it takes for most masculine faces to resemble feminine ones is astonishing, whether temporary or permanent. This truly underscores the profound differences between men and women and how it is no simple task to just switch from one to the other for most people.

One interesting dynamic that goes beyond physical transition is the impact on brain structures. In my own case, I know my natural testosterone levels are dramatically low and have been since I was first tested in high school.

Around the age of fifteen, my dad, sister and I stumbled upon one of those model searches at a mall that were so popular at the time. While my sister was the interested party, the organizers asked me to walk for them and to my sister's dismay and permanent resentment, they chose me to continue to the next step. The only barrier was my weight. I was my adult height of 6'1, but I was just over 100lbs. They decided I needed to *lose* some of that weight.

This sent me down a body dysmorphic spiral that crashed into severe anorexia and brief hospitalization. Having fallen under 100lbs, the doctors nearly kept me against my will, threatening to force-feed me with a tube if necessary. As part of their shock therapy approach, they reported my testosterone levels were extremely low and argued it was the anorexia.

Had my testosterone levels been extremely low since puberty or was it the result of malnutrition? I have often wondered if my lack of masculine instinct was biological, since it seemed to begin before socialization. Many would agree with that argument.

A 2019 study published in, *Neuropsychopharmacology*, for example argues, "Gonadal steroid increases and fluctuations during peri-puberty and across the reproductive lifespan influence the brain structure and function programmed by testosterone and estradiol exposures in utero."

The study confirms that there are clear differences between male and female brain activity, development and cognition beginning in utero through young adulthood. One hypothesis is that there is some unknown factor that interrupts the progress between physical development and brain development while in utero arguing a "disconnect between an individual's brain "sex/gender" and the sex associated with their reproductive organs due to the relative maturation of these organs across gestation, with genital development completed in first trimester and brain development continuing throughout pregnancy." [See Figure 1 in Appendix]

There are studies that indicate differences in resting state and cognitive abilities in transgender people which are closer in comparison to their preferred gender than their birth sex. However, 1/4th of available studies provides conflicting data, indicating that test subjects show identical brain structure with those of their biological sex.

Studies that acknowledge whether or not a transgender subject has already undergone hormone therapy indicate a significant change in their brain structure due solely to hormones. The study states, "While sex hormones can exert an organizational influence on brain morphology during prenatal and peri-pubertal development, as discussed above, sex steroids can still affect the brain later in adulthood when the brain has fully developed."

While "puberty blockers" are growing in popularity to "pause" sex hormones and prevent them from making permanent changes to the physical body, the study argues it is unclear how this impacts the development of the brain and there is not enough information to know if the practice is safe in the short or long run.

There just isn't sufficient evidence of a before and after picture of brain development at any point in the individual's life that allow researchers to determine if measurable differences in male and female brain development and activity were already in place or the result of artificial intervention.[44]

A study in 2016, featured *in Nature Reviews Endocrinology* titled, *Cross-sex hormones alter grey matter structures,* argued conclusively, "the findings suggest that high doses of cross-sex hormones alter structures in the adult human brain."[45]

According to a 2019 article titled, *The largest study involving transgender people is providing long-sought insights about their health*, in the journal, *Nature*, argues, however, "Researchers debate what kind of differences — if any — exist between male and female brains, and many such studies have been poorly interpreted. But scientists who study gender issues think that the confusion could be partly the result of a simplistic view of sex and gender identity. "I don't think there is something like a male or female brain, but it's more a continuum," says Baudewijntje Kreukels, a neuroscientist at Amsterdam University Medical Center."

The same researchers as clarify, "When Kreukels' group scanned the brains of a group of 21 transgender boys who had recently begun testosterone treatment, they found that their brains look more like those of cisgender boys."[46]

A 2017 article in *Stanford Medicine*, titled, *Two minds: The cognitive differences between men and women*, noted, "Many of these cognitive differences appear quite early in life. "You see sex differences in spatial-visualization ability in 2- and 3-month-old infants," Halpern says. Infant girls respond more readily to faces and begin talking earlier. Boys react earlier in infancy to experimentally induced perceptual discrepancies in their visual environment. In adulthood, women remain more oriented to faces, men to things."

The article continued, "Brain-imaging studies indicate that these differences extend well beyond the strictly reproductive domain, Cahill says. Adjusted for total brain size (men's are bigger), a woman's hippo-campus, critical to learning and memorization, is larger than a man's and works differently. Conversely, a man's amygdala, associated with the experiencing of emotions and the recollection of such experiences, is bigger than a woman's."

Women retain stronger and more viscerally emotional memories of events than men do, and their memories are more intense and detailed. The two hemispheres in a woman's brain talk to each other more frequently and easily than a man's. Men's brains tend to focus activity within specialized regions whereas women coordinate more widely from both sides.

Hormones impact this distinction as, "males developing normally in utero get hit with a big mid-gestation surge of testosterone, permanently shaping not only their body parts and proportions but also their brains. (Genetic defects disrupting testosterone's influence on a developing male human's cells induce a shift to a feminine body plan, our "default" condition.)"

Our sex chromosomes impact these changes as well, "A gene on the Y chromosome is responsible for the cascade of developmental events that cause bodies and brains to take on male characteristics. Some other genes on the Y chromosome may be involved in brain physiology and cognition."[47]

An article in *Time* magazine titled, *Transgender Men See Sexism From Both Sides*, reported the experiences of transgender men,

> *Those who had taken testosterone treatments said they noticed psychological changes that came with the medical transition. Most trans men said that after they took hormone treatments they felt more sure of themselves and slightly more aggressive than they had been before the treatment.*
>
> *"After transitioning I was able to think more clearly, I was more decisive," says the radio newscaster Gardner. He says the shift has affected his daily routine, even for something as ordinary as a trip to the grocery store. Before he transitioned, he says, he used to spend 45 minutes debating which pasta sauce to buy, which vegetables were the freshest. "I would stand there and look at the different varieties of yogurt," he recalls. "Now I just grab one. I'm looking for utility, I don't second-guess myself."*

> "As a female there was black and white and everything in between. When I started taking the hormones, it was more black and white," he explains, adding: "If I get into a disagreement with someone at work, I don't have that feeling afterwards of, 'I hope I didn't hurt his or her feelings.' I'm not a worrier as much as I was in the female body."[48]

This type of research is not limited to gender identity. A 2008 article in *National Geographic*, titled, *Brains of gay people resemble those of straight people of opposite sex*, states, "Ivanka Savic and Per Lindstrom at the Karolinska Institute in Stockholm scanned the brains of 90 men and women of different sexual orientations. Their images show that in the brains of gay people, certain features including symmetry and connections to the brain's emotional centre are more closely matched to the brains of straight people from the opposite sex."

The article continues, "Earlier studies have found similar results for patterns of brain activity. For example, parts of the brain involved in reward and emotion are more strongly activated when straight men and lesbian women look at female faces, and when straight women and gay men see male faces. The same patterns apply when people smell chemicals that probably act as human pheromones. But attractive faces and enticing pheromones are both related to sex, and responses to them could be learned over time."

Stating that these findings are likely developed before birth, "The idea that straight men have more asymmetrical brains than gay men fits with previous research. When listening to sounds, straight men tend to have a bias for their right ear, which both gay men and straight women lack. They also tend to outperform gay men and straight women in tests of spatial awareness, where success depends on a part of the brain – the parietal cortex – which is usually larger in men than in women."

As noted in studies on sex differences in the brain, "the amygdalas of gay men had more in common with those of straight women – the two halves were well-connected, they had more neurons projecting from the left half (as opposed to the right in straight men) and these neurons connected to the same parts of the brain that those of straight women do."

Could homosexual behavior in animals provide insight? The article states, "In animals, homosexuality in females is often attributed to an overabundance of male hormones – androgens – in the womb, while male homosexuality results from a lack of these. In male monkeys and rats, the right side of the brain has higher concentrations of receptors for these male hormones to lock onto; in females, they are distributed equally among the two halves."[49]

When considered together, it is curious to see how gender identity and sexual orientation could be linked. Studies on sexual orientation, as well as differences in biological sex, do not seem to hesitate in arguing clear distinctions in brain development. This is not presented as being clear when studying transgender brains.

Of course, it is far easier to study the brains of typically gendered men and women, gay or straight. Transgender studies are inherently restricted by necessary co-factors not present in the other groups. Transgender subjects, as indicated by available data, have already been influenced by sex hormones.

As I reported in 2021, transgender activists have begun aggressively blocking efforts of researchers to study brain development prior to hormone influence.

> The University of California at Los Angeles's Semel Institute for Neuroscience and Human Behavior was preparing a National Institute of Health-backed study to better understand brain structures and responses among people living with gender dysphoria. The study was titled, "Gender identity and own body perception – implications for

> *the neurobiology of gender dysphoria." Its researchers were seeking transgender participants when LGBT activists demanded the study be shut down.*
>
> *According to the physicians attempting to conduct the study, "We want to understand the neurobiology of gender dysphoria and the interactions between sex hormone therapy treatment, the brain, and the body phenotype." However, the executive director of the local activist group Gender Justice LA objected, claiming the study "opens the door for advancing the highly disregarded and dangerous practice of conversion therapy."*

Activists argued that the possibility of a transgender person discovering their brains did not conform to ideas of sex-segregated differences might "trigger" them and invalidate their experiences. Prior to the study, transgender activists began aggressively warning their peers to stay away from the study, declaring it "dangerous.

"We object to the view that transgender people have an aberrant body image condition or that brain imaging of traumatic response could ultimately 'help' trans people," the group wrote in the letter. "It is suggestive of a search for medical 'cure,' which can open the door for more gatekeeping and restrictive policies and practices in relation to access to gender-affirming care. At a time in which trans lives are under attack, we find this kind of research to be misguided and dangerous."[50]

Without sufficient study of brain development in those who believe they are transgender or who suffer from gender dysphoria, prior to hormone intervention, there simply will be no way to validate the argument of inherent brain development differences. As more children are placed on puberty blockers and then given cross-sex hormones, the ability to study this objectively will become even less viable.

If science can determine my brain looks like a woman's brain, does that validate my homosexuality or does that indicate I am a woman trapped in a man's body? Has my gender dysphoria been an awareness of female brain differences as compared to my male peers this whole time? Did embracing my sexual orientation fully allow me to abandon my sense of being the wrong gender?

Science does not currently have these answers and the information is conflicting. For example, there is no test for homosexuality or gender dysphoria based on brain scans. If there were, all transgender individuals could be medically screened for a measurable condition requiring specific medical intervention.

All homosexual men are not women in male bodies, however. The fact that study participants indicate similarities between gay men and women in brain structure and behavioral and cognitive function does not account for masculine gay men who are indistinguishable in behavior and self-awareness as straight men.

Are bisexual people a blend of both and if so, how is that brain development structured? According to the research, the distinctions come in terms of size, density and usage when performing neutral tasks. Do bisexual people have an equal distribution between the two, making them both male and female, from the point of view of the brain?

Another layer of complexity is the reality not all transgender people are attracted to the opposite sex. Both males and females who transition to the opposite sex, maintain their heterosexual orientation after transition. In the original documentary I mentioned, the man being followed through his transition was straight.

In the narrative he discussed how after fully transitioning, he tried to date men but couldn't force himself to be attracted to men, despite his difficulty in finding women who were now interested in him as a woman. Although he transitioned well and felt happy and secure in living as a woman, his sexual orientation did not change and was more difficult to adapt to his new life.

Viewing distress or confusion surrounding gender identity as a consequence of social intolerance rather than a symptom of a psychological disorder is another fundamental argument. This has been popularized in recent years as advocates within the psychological and medical communities have moved from understanding gender dysphoria as a condition to positioning it as a side effect. Rather than considering a person's incongruent perception of gender as itself a disorder, they argue that people born with, or born as, unique or divergent genders are forced into psychological distress due to intolerance and ignorance.

The APA states, "A person's identification as TGNC can be healthy and self-affirming, and is not inherently pathological. However, people may experience distress associated with discordance between their gender identity and their body or sex assigned at birth, as well as societal stigma and discrimination." This is where advocacy for the affirmation of TGNC identity rather than viewing the incongruence itself as a condition that needs to be medically resolved.

"Between the late 1960s and the early 1990s, healthcare to alleviate gender dysphoria largely reinforced a binary conceptualization of gender. At that time, it was considered an ideal outcome for TGNC people to conform to an identity that aligned with either sex assigned at birth or, if not possible, with the "opposite" sex, with a heavy emphasis on blending into the cisgender population or "passing", Interestingly, during the mid-20th century, a person who expressed severe distress over their physical sex would be recommended the path of a "sex-change."

The majority of laws and advocacy from the then transsexual and transvestite community focused on legal recognition of this surgical change and they were largely successful. However, modern medical perception appears to be moving away from this goal as an ideological mission.

The APA guideline on transgender care argues, "Variance from these options could raise concern for health care providers about a TGNC person's ability to transition successfully. These concerns could act as a barrier to accessing surgery or hormone therapy because medical and mental health care provider endorsement was required before surgery or hormones could be accessed,"[1] Variance indicates that a person did not consider themselves fully male or female, which would beg the question of why they would be interested in chemically and surgically changing their sex.

The argument against "gatekeeping" has been a primary advocacy position for some time. The idea being that in previous generations, a person was able to fully transition to the opposite sex and live as that sex with full legal recognition, but they had to submit to psychological evaluation and be approved first. This was done to prevent a person from rushing into a decision that might not have been right for them.

In a 1977 issue of *Drag* magazine, a magazine dedicated to transsexuals and transvestites, the story of a transsexual named Romaine Atura was reported under the headline, *Post-Op Transsexual Commits Suicide, Operation Was a Mistake!* The young man was described as going from an "effeminate homosexual, to transvestite, to drag queen to finally transsexual."

The article describes Atura's transition history stating, "Among the many things she questioned was her own psychiatric evaluation. A psychiatrist, recommended by one of New York City's most prominent sex change doctors, approved the surgery after only a 45-minute interview."

The article continued, "She herself had some doubts, and it seemed odd that this man could sort out in 45 minutes what she had been trying to figure for some twenty or so years. She was aware of how she had been coached by her friends and herself, seeking a final answer, as to say what to get over during the interview. She was aware that she had been spouting phrases that she had read, or heard, about transsexuals. She was confused as to whether or not she had been sincere or merely reading a script.

Even that could have been dealt with, following some in-depth interviews. But Romaine couldn't separate herself from her social environment – the drag bar. Peer pressure worked on her thought processes. She was confused and as such vulnerable to a "pat" answer. In her own circle of friends, the sex change was the peak of the social order. After all, isn't Christine [Jorgensen] on national TV regularly, and how nice it is not to be thought of as a "fag."

Her friends insisted by their attitudes and ignorance that she complete her surgery. After all, she was living as a woman, after all she had breasts, after all she wasn't a man. All those after all's convinced her she had to have a vagina. She she consented. She became a bit apprehensive when she had to sign a release absolving the doctor from all responsibility after surgery. But the only way to be finally sure was to go ahead and pray she had been right to take this chance.

She wasn't. Within a month of surgery, Romaine was back at the doctor, asking to have her penis restored, if possible. She just had no sensation in that hole. The doctor, who had so readily accepted her for reassignment surgery, agreed to try. But Romaine couldn't face another possible mistake. She threw herself off a building rather than accept this failure."[51]

The modern APA argument suggests that such barriers are harmful, "TGNC people have routinely been asked to obtain an endorsement letter from a psychologist attesting to the stability of their gender identity as a prerequisite to access an endocrinologist, surgeon, or legal institution (ie: Driver's License). The need for such required documentation from a psychologist may influence rapport, resulting in TGNC people fearing prejudicial treatment in which this documentation is withheld or delayed by the treating provider." Despite this, the guidelines insist, "Psychologists are encouraged to provide written affirmations supporting TGNC people and their gender identity so that they may access necessary services (e.g., hormone therapy)."[1]

In a 1976 issue of *Drag*, there was an article detailing a doctor who had performed more than hundred sex-change operations who began arguing against them as a therapeutic practice. "An endocrinologist named Dr. Charles L. Ihlenfeld, who was an openly gay man, argued, "Nonpsychiatric professionals, including myself, have tended to see themselves as rescuers." Discussing a recent study he stated, "whatever surgery did, it did not fulfill a basic yearning for something that is difficult to define. This goes along with the idea that we are trying to treat superficially something that is much deeper. It may also mean that if you are born to be a transsexual, you are doomed never to be totally happy."[52]

These examples shed light on just how long this conflict has been burdening those suffering with gender confusion or dysphoria and how the medical field has never been quite sure how to handle it. The influence of activism has only made matters worse, with the stories of those who transitioned, only to detransition later being ignored or dismissed entirely from the conversation.

For example, NBC News reported on this issue stating, "trans advocates say some of the recent coverage around the topic portrays detransitioning as much more common than it actually is, fueling misconceptions about the gender transition process and painting trans people as just temporarily confused or suffering from a misdiagnosed psychological disorder. This misleading information, they say, can have serious real-world consequences, from misguided policy proposals to social stigma."

The article continued, "I think the reason why detransition stories are popular in this given time is because it neatly fits into this idea that young people especially are being made to be trans,"

Lui Asquith, a legal counselor for U.K.-based LGBTQ group Mermaids, told NBC News. "The media are conjuring up a panic about trans lives, and the first victims of that panic are the young people who are indirectly being told that they're a phase."[53]

A 2021 study published in the journal, LGBT Health, titled, Factors Leading to "Detransition" Among Transgender and Gender Diverse People in the United States: A Mixed-Methods Analysis, reported that in a study of 17,151 transgender individuals, 13 percent (2,242) had detransitioned.

The study, however, attributed these cases to, "Frequently endorsed external factors included pressure from family and societal stigma. History of detransition was associated with male sex assigned at birth, nonbinary gender identity, bisexual sexual orientation, and having a family unsupportive of one's gender identity. A total of 15.9% of respondents reported at least one internal driving factor, including fluctuations in or uncertainty regarding gender identity."[54]

Along with these assumptions, the APA has adopted the intersectional construct, a social theory in which all of society is categorized by privilege and oppression. They argue, "Gender identity and gender expression may have profound intersections with other aspects of identity. These aspects may include, but are not limited to, race/ethnicity, age, education, socioeconomic status, immigration status, occupation, disability status, HIV status, sexual orientation, relational status, and religion and/or spiritual affiliation. Whereas some of these aspects of identity may afford privilege, others may create stigma and hinder empowerment."

How is this understood, they state, "To illustrate, an African American trans man may gain male privilege, but may face racism and societal stigma particular to African American men. An Asian American/Pacific Islander trans woman may experience the benefit of being perceived as a cisgender woman, but may also experience sexism, misogyny, and objectification particular to Asian American/Pacific Islander cisgender women."

Further they consider the impact of perceived oppression, "Discrimination can include assuming a person's assigned sex at birth is fully aligned with that person's gender identity, not using a person's preferred name or pronoun, asking TGNC people inappropriate questions about their bodies, or making the assumption that psychopathology exists given a specific gender identity or gender expression."

Rather than approaching the topic from a medical perspective, treating a condition with the goal of a specific outcome, the discussion has become buried under layers of social theory that is inherently hostile to objective study.

Despite acknowledging that study sizes were small and not representative of population data, the guidelines instruct, "Psychologists recognize that TGNC people are more likely to experience positive life outcomes when they receive social support or trans-affirmative care." They justify this by reporting, "In a meta-analysis of the hormone therapy treatment literature with TGNC adults and adolescents, researchers reported that 80% of participants receiving trans-affirmative care experienced an improved quality of life, decreased gender dysphoria, and a reduction in negative psychological symptoms."[1]

The study cited, *Hormonal therapy and sex reassignment: a systematic review and meta-analysis of quality of life and psychosocial outcomes*, reviewed 28 studies covering 1833 patients who underwent reassignment surgery that included hormone therapy, nearly half male to female and female to male. The APA statement implies that hormone therapy alone was the baseline. The study did find that 80 percent of individuals with Gender Identity Disorder, as it was known in 2010, reported, "significant improvement in gender dysphoria." That same percentage also reported improvement in their quality of life, and 72 percent said they saw improvement in their sexual function.

However, the study concluded stating, "Very low quality evidence suggests that sex reassignment that includes hormonal interventions in individuals with GID likely improves gender dysphoria, psychological functioning and comorbidities, sexual function and overall quality of life." The report also stated "All the studies were observational and most lacked controls." All evidence was self-reported.[55]

In spite of this, the guidelines insist, "Given the strong evidence for the positive influence of affirmative care, psychologists are encouraged to facilitate access to and provide trans-affirmative care to TGNC people. Whether through the provision of assessment and psychotherapy, or through assisting clients to access hormone therapy or surgery, psychologists may play a critical role in empowering and validating TGNC adults' and adolescents' experiences and increasing TGNC people's positive life outcomes."[1] This statement was sited from a 2009 study titled, *The Experiences of Transgendered Persons in Psychotherapy: Voices and Recommendations.*

The study recruited seven transgender individuals who had been seeing their therapist for the majority of three months while living as the opposite sex. After conducting interviews, the study reported, "Results suggest that the participants did not experience many of the heterosexist, sexist, and pathologizing biases described in previous studies. Rather, they described supportive and affirming relationships with their therapists. Some participants had had negative experiences with previous therapists. Participants called for further training and education for therapists and other helping professionals. Implications for theory, research, practice, and policy are explored."[56]

The prospect of transitioning and living a full life as the opposite sex has been distorted by politics, social theory, activism and an insatiable demand from LGBT organizations to present a preferred outcome rather than an objective truth. While the available options for pursing transition have never been more attainable and publicly validated, the consequences of the decision are often intentionally withheld and denied by the highest and most trusted authorities in the field.

Based on the available research and self-reported feedback from other transgender people, I can now better understand how this choice would have impacted my life. As female hormones restructured my brain and my testosterone levels artificially suppressed, it is very possible I may have experienced the transition in a positive way.

The change in perspective, either enhancing my already feminine brain or forcing my male brain to feminize, would have distorted my before and after consideration, similar to how those who suffer from depression, anxiety or bipolar disorder experience a change after taking medications.

It is also possible that cosmetic changes might have been interpreted differently with a more feminized brain than imagined by current perspective. Perhaps the physical transition wouldn't have been as difficult or distressing as I feared. Just as the man who inspired my journey discovered in his own transition to living as a woman, adapting to my new life circumstances would have been challenging, but perhaps not impossible.

I have to consider, however, that these changes would be entirely artificial. Unlike medications designed to alter the chemical makeup of my brain to reduce depression and anxiety, effectively providing me a reasonably normal chemical composition and allowing me to perceive the world from a healthier perspective, hormones would simply alter my brain artificially.

Would this really be a gateway into finding my authentic self, or would it be the creation of a new perspective, forced by hormones rather than my own mind? The idea that my physical brain structure could be permanently altered to better accommodate my inner sense of gender, rather than correcting my body to better align with my gender was, and is, disturbing.

Similar to the difference between medications designed to correct brain chemical imbalances and those designed to artificially increase or decrease chemicals to achieve a specific desired outcome, transition would have created a lifelong dependance on treatment. I wouldn't have been freed from a medical condition causing me to suffer, I would simply have intervened in my natural development to create a preferred outcome, one that would be inherently unsustainable.

I experienced this distinction when my doctor prescribed me medication to quell my panic attacks. The medication altered my body's nerve system response by increasing chemicals higher than they would otherwise be. In doing so, my brain, over time, would stop creating these chemicals altogether and if I stopped taking the medication, would be unable to regulate that system on its own.

This created a dependance on that medication, as removing it from my system would not only cause severe withdrawl symptoms, it would leave my brain unable to defend itself from the underlying cause of my panic attacks, making them more debilitating.

Men who take testosterone recreationally to artificially increase athletic performance and muscle mass experience this consequence as well, losing their ability to create their own hormone. Pretending that this type of medical intervention excludes transgender people is, in my opinion, deeply troubling.

After all the research and experience I can find, I can't help but feel the transgender transition state is itself artificial and merely creates the illusion of fulfillment through artificial medical and chemical intervention. If I became reliant on medical treatment to preserve the transition, continuously fighting my body's relentless attempts to revert back to its natural state, I am not confident that would have been the life I was hoping to live.

Worse, if I lost the ability to even understand what changes had been made, I feel it would have been an assault on my own autonomy rather than a life-saving solution, validating my lifelong determination to become something I objectively was not.

Eight

Life

No matter how much I wanted the outcome, or thought I did at least, I couldn't waste any more of my life pursuing the impossible. College had changed my outlook. I believed for the first time that I had a future. I was optimistic and I didn't want anything to hold me back. I decided I couldn't keep chasing a dream that only kept me from waking up and living my life.

I was still deeply dissatisfied, however, with my interactions with gay men and my sexual encounters. I was beginning to change physically, growing more facial hair and my body was starting to fill out. I struggled to pull off the 'twink' persona and the men most interested in it noticed. I started getting rejected for being too old and too masculine looking. The men I was most attracted to, older, masculine, lager men, who often referred to themselves as 'daddies,' wanted a 'boy' they could dominate and treat as a girlfriend. I was becoming less and less attractive to them every day.

In my experiences online there were a limited number of options a gay man could fit into. Outside of 'twink,' the remaining options involved ever-increasing levels of masculinity, or at least the presentation of masculinity. Since I would never be a big hairy man and I couldn't fake athletic interest to save my life, I realized my only choice was to become more masculine, any way I could.

I certainly found it ironic that the desperate struggle of my youth, to be more like the other boys, had become the defining challenge of my young adult life. Even as a gay man I couldn't escape the demands of masculinity. The difference now was that I didn't have to fake interest or participate in activities I hated, I just had to look the part. I just needed to workout.

The internal struggle was complex as I approached the realization that I could never turn back if I started down this path. If I wouldn't be able to transition with the tall skinny body I already had, wouldn't adding muscular definition and bulk make things worse if I ever decided to, or had the opportunity to, reconsider my decision? Every time I lifted weights, I felt like I was betraying a part of myself, bullying that small, scared child inside to be quiet and disappear forever.

This conflict typically repeated itself over and over as I would begin going to the gym, feel overwhelmed with guilt and insecurity, abandon the idea, and then restart it again after beating myself up for stopping. It seemed no matter what I did, there was nowhere for me to fit in.

I had straight male friends and I was a perpetual joke to them, one I allowed and encouraged. I had a lot of pressure from my straight girlfriends to be the gay man they thought I should be, and gay men were either dismissive of my lack of masculinity or rejected me outright for being too masculine for their tastes.

All the while, I hid all of this from my family, who had essentially moved on with their lives as I toiled in obscurity, hidden away in my apartment. I had broached the subject of transition with my dad once while we were living together in a rare moment of mutual clarity. Every so often, my relationship as his therapist would resurface and I would spend long hours coaching him out of dark places and spirals of despair.

In this particular occasion, feeling emboldened by my reasonably positive recent experience with my grandparents, I took a chance and told him the same thing I told them. Rather than anger or disgust, or even avoidance, he just sort of slumped into himself, his face flattening as his greatest fear seemed to be coming true before his eyes. With tears building up he only whispered out, weakly with clear and painful defeat, "But you're my baby boy."

I never brought it up again. We never talked about these things. He had long chosen to avoid the reality rather than embrace it and I was more than happy to indulge him. As I approached my mid-twenties, a time when as a child I once imagined I would be married and celebrating the birth of my first child, that avoidance nearly killed me.

I was working as a busboy and hating absolutely every minute of it. At $7.00 an hour, however, it was the highest paying job I ever had, and I was on my own and in college, so I forced my way through it. A few weeks in, though, my biggest barrier was not my personal distaste for the work, but the physical labor of the work itself. My job was to scurry around the restaurant with an oversized platter, fill it with every item on the table left over from the guests and rush it back to the kitchen for cleaning.

Never brave enough to hoist the platter full of plates, glasses, and other assorted dinner accessories up to my shoulder and carry it to the back like the others, I frequently carried it with both hands at waist level. I was told this was harder and more tiring, but in my mind, it was my only option, and I wasn't about to have an embarrassing public accident and cover myself with the leftovers and shattered wine glasses of recent diners.

One day, though, the task was more difficult than the day before. Every repeated movement from a table to the back caused all my joints to ache and left me feeling dizzy and out of breath. The discomfort only grew worse and within a week I was collapsing in the employee bathroom, crying at the pain and fear of what was happening to me. My grandmother's husband laughed it off as an amusing life lesson on hard work. I wasn't so convinced.

The pain in my joints quickly turned into pain in my stomach and I woke up one night with the intense urge to vomit. I didn't stop for several hours. I fell asleep on my bathroom floor and woke up the next day an hour late for my evening shift. I didn't have a phone and so I somehow managed to gather the strength to get up, walk a block to the nearest phone booth and call my manager to explain that I was too sick to come in that day. They were less than sympathetic.

The vomiting only got worse and when I looked in the mirror, my skin was a pale yellow, and so were my eyes. I managed to get myself to the hospital, after another day of violent sickness and sitting in the waiting room I felt profoundly alone. The doctor determined I was suffering from hepatitis. The test came back with hepatitis B and there was nothing they could do. I would get better on my own, or, possibly, wouldn't.

My dad was alerted of my condition when the health department reached out to him as my emergency contact and told him I had to come in for evaluation. He showed up at my door and with great frustration and clear disappointment, took me to the office. Hepatitis B is a sexually transmitted disease and so the health department needed me to list my previous sexual partners.

I sat there, with my father who was looking down and away from me the entire time, and fumbled my way through the questions, carefully editing every word. When we were finished, he drove me home and as I got out of the car he simply said, "You did this to yourself," and drove off. My grandparents weren't much better. They too considered this a punishment from God for my reckless, deviant behavior, behavior they assumed I was engaging in of course. Ironically, in the months prior, I had gone through a dry spell. When I tried to plead innocence that I didn't know how I had been exposed, my grandmother sharply responded, "You know how you got it."

The illness worsened and I was forced to quit my job. I obviously couldn't work in a restaurant, and I had become too sick to do much of anything but lay helplessly on my makeshift bed in my one room apartment and crawl to the bathroom. I managed to get to class though, spending the hours between them huddled in the corner of the handicap stall.

The worst night of the illness I had an epiphany that would change the course of my life. As I stared at the ceiling, fully believing I would die that night, I prayed and let go of everything I ever cared or worried about. I felt truly helpless and in a way that was comforting. I didn't have to try anymore. I waited for whatever I imagined the moment would be like and I accepted it fully. I drifted off to sleep. The next morning, I woke up feeling a little embarrassed, a little confused and surprisingly better.

The days that followed showed improvement and soon my eyes and skin returned to normal. My doctor reported a stressed, but functioning liver and I quickly found a new job. How sick I actually was I will never know, but in my mind, I believed I was at the brink of death that night and had a new opportunity to change my life. I decided to take it.

As I progressed in school and settled into the routine of two jobs, a new, bigger apartment, a new kitten to occupy my attention and a stronger confidence in a new and exciting spirituality, the life I left seemed much less important. I still visited my grandparents regularly and my dad, now married and being taken care of by someone else, had become less of a mental burden for me. The question of whether or not I should become a woman seemed further away.

My world, once again, endured a seismic quake when my father was suddenly rushed to the hospital suffering from a heart attack. His condition dramatically worsened and within hours he was prepped for surgery, a quadruple bypass. I chose to spend that evening at his new home, a cute doublewide trailer built into the side of a large hill in the valley of two mountains, where his new wife and her former husband lived.

At night in the withering summer, the air was alive with life. The woods just beyond the boundary of their yard promised secrets and beckoned exploration. The open sky along with the seemingly endless sounds of tiny creatures singing to one another gave the feeling of pure abandonment. It was uniquely magical. Alone, I sat outside, staring at the night sky, and waited for the call, one I knew was coming. I had been preparing for that call my entire life.

He hated his father, who had long ago given up on a life outside of work and drinking, and on more than one occasion he prevented his father from setting himself, or the house, on fire after passing out with a lit cigarette in his hand. He was very close to his mother, though, and they protected each other from his father's drunken outbursts of violence and rage.

His sister was older and ventured out on her own the moment she had the chance, got married and seemingly never looked back, keeping a careful distance between her new life and her old one. My dad never left his mother. He dedicated his life to her, trying to be the husband she never had. As a child he would comfort her when she cried after a fight, and he often took beatings that were meant for her. As he entered his adult life, his days were scheduled around his mother's needs.

He managed his bottled-up rage by releasing it in acts of teenage recklessness. My father had been a reckless and heroic-minded young man, despite his battle with severe depression and paranoia. As a young teenager he and his friends joined his uncle's volunteer fire department.

While still in high school he decided to show off for his friends by putting a firetruck in neutral and allowing it to roll down a small hill, where he jumped out and ran behind it, attempting to prove he could stop it by himself. The cheers of his friends were quickly replaced with horrified shouts, however, when he overestimated his strength, and the firetruck ran him over.

Never defeated by such things, he reported that at the hospital, where he almost lost his right leg, he gleefully assisted the doctor in holding open his wound when the nurse became too sick to continue. He desperately wanted to be known for his bravery and heroics and his one shining moment came when he was a senior in high school, and he saved two of his fellow high school volunteer firemen from a flood that made the local papers.

But over time that glory faded. His athletic career had been cut short due to his injury and he became a bystander watching his friends move on with their own lives and triumphs. He fell into a deep depression and attempted suicide on multiple occasions, several times nearly successfully. He would tell me he always fought his way back from the edge because he couldn't leave his mother alone with his father.

Shortly after high school he met my mother who had recently moved to the area and joined his former high school as a junior. My dad was still friends with lower classman, and he quickly charmed her, as he did every woman he ever met. She saw him as a way to escape her abusive mother and he saw her as his chance to prove himself to his father that he was a man and could take on real responsibility.

My mother told me she cried on her wedding day because she was so young and didn't know my father at all. He was the first boy who noticed her, and she realized she was marrying a stranger. My dad was too busy trying to make his parents proud to notice. They moved into a small trailer together, purchased by his parents, and while she moved from one abusive relationship to another, he found himself quickly bored with domestic life.

He enjoyed frightening her. He encouraged her separation from her family and then began strictly enforcing it. Within months of their marriage, she was entirely isolated in her home, under the unforgiving eye of my grandmother who deeply disapproved of her, and the unpredictable hand of my father. As she would later recount, and he often enjoyed boasting to me about, his only moments of happiness at home were when he was terrorizing her.

He loved to tell her of all the ways he could murder her and dispose of her body without anyone ever knowing. He would randomly speed up his car and drive recklessly, laughing as she screamed, telling her he could kill them both at any moment. He would invite his friends over and allow them to do as they pleased with her. He would leave for the evening and then return with a mask on, sneak in through the window and then rape her. That was how I was conceived.

The surprise pregnancy calmed things for my mother and when I was born it seemed she had finally achieved a level of approval from her new family. As she was forbidden to speak to her own, they didn't even know she had given birth until I was six months old. She profoundly loved me and saw me as her only escape from my father's cruelty. A little over a year later, she became pregnant again, and soon had a toddler and a newborn to occupy her time.

It seems my father resented both the attention from his mother towards me and the unexpected joy and tenderness his father suddenly expressed towards his new grandson. One Sunday morning when I was two, he was the one who put me into my car seat and as my mother and grandmother would later tell me, he was driving particularly recklessly that day.

They were on their way to church, his uncle on his mother's side was the pastor, and he took a turn more sharply than usual. My mother didn't realize what happened until she saw him staring intensely in the rearview mirror and turned to see my car seat upside down on the road behind them and my small body crumbled next to it.

Forcing him to stop she and others ran to the car seat and found me unconscious, face-down on the road with the back of my head bleeding. The official story was that I unbuckled myself, climbed out of the seat and opened the door just as my dad took the turn.

My mother became paranoid that my father would kill us all and she tried to tell anyone who would listen, but in this small town, everyone knew my father and dismissed it. He, of course, was told his of crazy wife spreading insane rumors and she would pay dearly for it when he came home. My mother told me he became obsessed with serial killers and began buying books and magazines on true crime, leaving them out for her see.

In my own experience with him, I can confirm this is true. He was mesmerized by body horror, watched nothing but horror movies and collected true crime books and magazines. His fascination stayed with him his entire life. The first books and movies I had access to were his collection of body horror media.

When my sister turned one, my mother and my father's former best friends ran away together. They were stopped by police officers, friends of my father's, one he had been close to since high school, and prevented from getting too far away. My mother, however, had made up her mind and with the help of her family and her new boyfriend, filed for divorce. She agreed to take my sister and leave me, believing if I was with my grandparents, I would be safe, and truthfully, it was the only deal they were willing to make.

He told everyone my sister wasn't really his, but his best friend's child, and she and he had run away, abandoning me. The story would eventually evolve to report they had all died in a car accident on their way out of town, a story both my father and grandmother felt would be the easiest way for me to understand and allow me to avoid the stigma of being a child of divorce.

Raising me as a single father, my dad again quickly grew bored of domestic life and longed to recapture his heroic youth. Although I have no memory of my life before the age of seven, many witnesses at the time, and my father on occasion, told me of the unusual number of times he rescued me from severe danger, typically on the job as a fireman.

He would, as I understand, take me to the scene of a house fire and tell me there was a kitten inside that I needed to rescue. He would then bravely risk his own life to enter the blaze to pull me back out, frequently reporting me as a different child. He would live off this rush and the adulation of his peers for a while until it faded and then he would find another dangerous situation to rescue me from.

I spent a great deal of time in the hospital at this age, I always seemed to be sick or injured. Finally, at around age five, my grandparents insisted I be left with my grandfather's brother, the fire chief, if my dad had to go out on a call. They would eventually demand he wake them up and bring me to them. My grandmother would go on to buy the house next door so that my father and I could be as close to her as possible to keep an eye on.

My first available memories of my father are at around age seven or so and they involve me pleading for him not to harm himself or leave me. As my dad got older, his suicidality and his reckless behavior increased. He was always dating someone, often multiple women at a time, and I had grown accustomed to telling people that I just didn't have a mom. I considered my grandmother to be my mom and acted accordingly with every Mother's Day celebration or gift project at school.

Alone with my dad, however, I became his outlet for all the emotions he kept inside. Despite my fear of him, I felt a great obligation to care for him, believing his pain to be my failure. I knew I could save him, fix him, if I just tried hard enough. I called 911 on more than one occasion to save him from an overdose or him cutting himself with a knife. I felt responsible for him.

By the time that evening arrived, with me staring out at the wide-open nothingness of country sky, that feeling of obligation had grown weary. I fantasized repeatedly of picking up the phone and hearing that he didn't survive his surgery. I wanted him to die, even if I felt guilty for thinking it. I wanted it to be over. I had spent my life trying to save him and I was neglecting my own.

He didn't die that night. He made a remarkable recovery, considering the seriousness of his condition. It had taken two nurses to break open his ribcage, he required four bypasses, and the surgeon almost lost him a few times. But he survived. He always seemed to survive. His recovery was painful, but for him, joyous.

A continuous stream of friends, some he hadn't seen since high school, came to visit him. The flow of care and concern filled him with euphoria. The high was incredible for him, and I'd never seen him glow the way he did in his hospital room for those few days. I stayed safely in the background, observing, unsure what to feel. I smiled and told him how happy I was for him and that I loved him, but secretly, I felt hollow.

I took care of him, along with his wife, when he went home and that incredible high, the highest he'd ever felt in his life, crashed down on all of us. As the good wishes and concerned affection dwindled, he found himself, once again, alone. He sat in his chair, stretched back, his head to the side and he stayed silent, softly crying and bitterly angry. He took his anger out on his new wife and, of course, me.

A few days later, as I was getting ready to leave for the evening, I told him I would see him the next day and that I loved him, with his head turned away he bitterly scoffed that I had ever loved him. This time, this one final time, I chose not to chase after him, pleading for him to accept my love. I just turned away and left. He died early the next morning from a drug overdose. He was 49.

He was obsessed with death. Deeply morbid and took great interest in and fascination with anything that disturbed and frightened others. He wished he'd become a mortician so he could do autopsies and one of his friends who was one, let him watch several to his great amusement. He took me along as well, he would later tell me, forcing me to see death as a way of trying to toughen me up.

Once while driving home from visiting my stepmother's family for Christmas, we got caught in traffic due to a severe car accident. It was snowing, late evening and the highway had been completely shut down. My father pulled out his emergency fire alert light and placed it on the roof of his car, indicating he was a trained official who could help.

He parked near the accident, and I remember looking out the window through intermittent swipes of snow and ice surrounded entirely by blue and red flashing lights. He'd jumped out to see if he could help, but there was nothing he could do. A man and woman in a van were driving too fast and she wasn't wearing her seatbelt, they hit an icy patch, slammed on the breaks, and she flew out the window and the van rolled over her body, landing upside down.

I know these details because within moments of rushing out to the scene, he came back, opened the side door and pulled me out to go along with him. I was used to this ritual. I was frequently with him at crashes, fires and other emergencies and he always pulled me in to get a closer look and to teach me about what was going on.

As the emergency crews and police officers were running around, helping the many other injured people who had been caught in the accident, my dad snuck me over along the side of the road and brought me close to the woman who had flown out of the window.

I was numb to these sorts of things and had been paying more attention to the beauty of heavy snow flooding the night sky, sparkling from the lights all around us. With a smack to the back of my head to get me to focus, I looked down and saw the woman, her face had been entirely crushed inward, her hair in a wide splash around her and her broken leg twisted unnaturally with one arm broken behind her back.

The image was seared into my mind instantaneously as my dad was excitedly demonstrating how the accident happened, and then silence, absolute nothingness fell over me. It felt like I had been pulled backwards into a black hole and my memory instantly stops. I came to again, gazing out the window at the snow as my dad drove away, lost in the euphoria of a manic high, detailing the scene and the crash and laughing at how big of a pussy I had been seeing the body.

Earlier in my life, my memory jumps to a moment where he was angrily shouting at me about something, I don't know remember what, and holding a small kitten near a broken area in a box fan with the blades turned on high. I was pleading for him to stop, and he kept inching the kitten's head closer to the opening.

Another flash and I am outside in our back yard looking down at the bloody remains of a kitten I had just killed with the brick still in my hand as he shouted behind me to stop crying. He'd forced me to do it, to prove I was a man, to beat the weakness out of me and all I could do was cry.

It was common in my rural area for boys as young as eight to kill be taken out into the woods with their father, uncles and brothers and kill their first deer. They would come to school afterwards bragging about the experience and I couldn't even imagine committing the act myself, to my father's frustration.

I had attempted to take my own life twice as a young teenager. I tried to cut my right wrist with a razor when I was 15, shaking so badly the wound was uneven. The scar is now covered by a tattoo. When my father discovered what I'd done, after I broke down in English class watching *Dead Poets Society* and revealed to my teacher what I'd done, he was angry that I had done it incorrectly.

The second time, I wandered out of my grandfather's house in a trance, walking down the long steep hill to the river where our neighbor had a deck that stretched far out into the water. Barefoot and shirtless, I shambled towards to the dock, walked to the water's edge, took off the rest of my clothing and stood naked, staring out at the night sky and dark, cold water.

Feeling as though I was already dead, a ghost watching the last moments of my life, I stepped out and fell into the water. The dark current instantly pulled me under and for a brief time I relived a moment when I was eleven and had almost drowned at the beach trying to save my sister who had ventured out too far into the ocean.

I only remember feeling movement, icy cold and a sense of pure abandon before I was roughly pulled out by several men further down the river who were sitting in their boat and drinking. They saw me in the water, and one dived in to rescue me, pulling me out and I was taken to the emergency room. I was 14 and they knew me and my grandfather. My dad didn't come to the hospital.

He always seemed so disappointed in my humanity, the fact that I couldn't find joy and pleasure in the morbidity he loved to indulge himself with. When I looked away at an accident or jumped at a scary movie, or cried at the loss of a pet, he lost hope in me ever being like him.

He loved to terrorize my sister and I in the same way he did my mother. One of his favorite games was to leave for the evening, park his car down the street and sneak to the house wearing a hockey mask and loudly starting up a chainsaw.

My stepmother often went to church in the evenings, and I was left responsible for watching my sister. Alone in the house, the two of us would hear the noises outside. He had instructed both of us many times on what to do during a home invasion, and hearing bangs against the house, I knew I had to keep my sister safe.

On one such occasion, she and I were watching TV when we caught a glimpse of movement outside, only to see a man wearing a hockey mask and holding a chainsaw staring at us through the window. I rushed her to a closet, shutting the door and instructing her to be quiet. I then ran to the phone to call 911, but the line was dead, he'd unplugged it before he left. He then revved up the chainsaw and I saw him peering through the backdoor, which wasn't locked.

Running to the door I managed to lock it just as he got to the window, staring down at me through the eye holes. I ran back to the closet with my sister who was huddled down crying softly, locked the door from the inside and covered us both with jackets. Then I heard the door loudly bang open.

He skulked around the house, escalating the terror, and then paused at the closet door. Reenacting his favorite movies, *Halloween* and *Friday the 13th*, he waited, silent, until suddenly grabbing the door handle and shaking it violently until it broke open.

Grabbing the jackets off us, my sister behind me as I blocked her as close to the wall as possible, he roared, revving the chainsaw again and she and I began desperately screaming. He then pulled the mask back revealing his face, laughing so hard he was crying and tried to calm us down.

He always argued he was just trying to prepare us for the real thing. I genuinely don't know what our neighbors thought, but I know my grandparents assumed it was just background noise in the small town where the sound of chainsaws was not uncommon. I still check the locks each night and secure the blinds, sometimes getting up multiple times to make sure they are still secure. I suppose in a way, his efforts worked.

When I got the call that he had died, it was early in the morning and as I drove up the long, winding hill to his house, the song, *What Hurts The Most*, by Rascal Flatts played on the radio. Numb and utterly overwhelmed, the song broke through me, causing a devastating dam of tears to burst through. I hadn't expected to cry.

Arriving to the house, the ambulance was just moving my father's body on a stretcher down the steps. Covered in a sheet, he seemed so small. His wife was standing in her robe, surrounded by her own family, all who lived within walking distance, and my grandmother was pacing along the deck, looking out into the early morning forest.

He'd wanted to be cremated, but my grandmother insisted on a traditional burial, one we couldn't afford, but I would eventually pay off on my own. His funeral reminded me very much of his hospital room, with dozens of people from his past crowding the room. One of my former classmates approached me and told me my father was a good man. He'd been a beloved coach to them.

I stood next to my grandmother and his devastated and terrified third wife, as my stepmother took her place at the other end. A steady stream of people passed by, but I only remember their faces, nothing else. It was surreal and I was lost in a perpetual sensation of loud buzzing vibration in my head.

My little brother, who was a young teenager and lived a dramatically different life with my father than I had, stood by his mother, staring off and awkwardly shuffling around. I hadn't been close to him. We had a 10-year gap between us, and I found him difficult to talk to.

On that day, though, I realized that my own pain and anger had prevented me from appreciating what my father meant to the world outside of me. My entire life I had positioned him in contrast to me and our relationship was adversarial. I never knew how much the other boys in my class and even several above and below me loved my father and how much he impacted their lives.

That evening I heard story after story of how his advice, encouragement and joyful presence had changed the lives of so many young men. He remained a volunteer fireman until his surgery, and he'd trained dozens of young men who looked up to him.

As a kid I remember how strange it was that the other boys knew my dad and would run up to him, shouting his first name with excited smiles. I would just stand there with a raised eyebrow confused as those same boys were my tormentors.

Standing there, seeing a room packed with people who only knew my father as a funny, loveable, dedicated hero, I felt more alone than I ever had in my life. Was I the only person who knew who he really was? I felt a profound obligation to preserve the memory his community held for him. I had to bury my feelings, my trauma and pain and let him live on as he wanted to be remembered in the minds of other people.

He received a traditional fireman's parade on the way to his burial. Being the oldest son, I stood with his coffin on my shoulder, leading the group of dedicated volunteers who all felt a sense of honor carrying him. I sat in the front of the leading car as it drove under multiple firetrucks, all with their ladders raised and flags displayed.

All of this was for him, it wasn't for me. It was if I hadn't existed in his life at all. His memory was owned by so many others that he didn't feel like he was my father, but theirs. At the funeral, his uncle spoke as I sat next to my grandmother who held my hand tightly. I remember he specifically stated that he knew he would never see his nephew again in Heaven, but he prayed for God's mercy in spite of that. My grandmother cried.

When it was all over, I gave my brother and sister one last hug, and I went back to the vehicle that brought me. That was the last I saw of them. I reasoned my duty to that family and to that part of our past was over now. I was free.

Life after my father was surreal. I had been on my own for some time, but he never quite left me. I was always close by to rush in and handle another crisis, another fight with his wife, another cycle of depression or suicidal threats. Suddenly, all of that was gone.

My father owned nothing. He had no belongings, nothing to remember him by. I don't have a single object he ever touched. I had one voicemail recording of his that I lost. It was almost as if he never lived at all.

Traumatized by her experience, his last wife changed the locks on the door the day of the funeral, changed her number and relocated. I never saw her again. In the last year of his life, he had reconnected with his mother, after decades of bitter separation. He blamed her for his marital strife with his second wife which eventually caused me to leave. He blamed her for his life turning out the way it did because he always believed she could rescue him, and she never did.

That last year a truce was formed, but it was never like it had been before. My father felt his mother owed him for years of suffering and she felt her son owed her an apology. I became the buffer between them. After he died, she had a lost look in her eyes. I saw her cry for only the second time in my life, the first being at her own mother's funeral when I was eight, and the second at her son's. Despite her ability to remain calm, logical, and emotionally distant, those walls had broken down some.

For me, I felt a profound sense of relief that I was ashamed to admit. The weight of him had been lifted and I ran away from the shadow as quickly as I could. I felt a new sense of freedom and possibility. In many ways, I had been avoiding a real relationship because I didn't want to deal with introducing a new partner to that life. I had begun exploring Judaism and felt a strong purpose in that path. I was defining the parameters of my life and I didn't need his permission or to suffer his disapproval any longer.

The last remaining thread to the life I had tried so very hard to leave behind me was my grandmother, and that too would soon end. It began innocently enough with my grandmother visiting her doctor complaining of neck pain, but it quickly escalated to a diagnosis of stage four bone cancer. She suffered with scoliosis her entire life, which is ironic considering everyone who knew her only ever saw her standing tall. Her back pain had haunted her for decades.

Somehow in all the years of tests, treatments, spinal taps and other various medical tortures she endured, no one noticed the growing cancer in her bones. By the time they found it, the bones in her in neck had degraded to such a point they were barely supporting her head. She came home in a neck brace with strict orders to remain as immobile as possible.

Just a week prior she had been in her garden, pulling weeds and admiring her abundance of flowers. A week after her diagnosis, she was in a hospital bed, barely conscious and ready to be moved to hospice. I got to spend one final night with her when I visited, and we realized her husband needed a break. I stayed up all night holding her hand.

Surprisingly, during the night she began to talk to me, in a sleepy dream like state, she told me of how proud she was of me and how deeply she loved me. She was so close to heaven, and she just wanted me to be there with her one day. She told me she had always regretted keeping me at a distance over my being gay. I forgave her and we shared a blissful moment of true spiritual bonding before she drifted off back to sleep.

I would never get to talk to her again, and a week later she passed. Her daughter, who like my father, held a deep resentment of my relationship with her parents, quickly took control and denied me even a single piece of my grandmother's jewelry. I had only asked for one necklace, a diamond shaped cameo she wore more days than not that I treasured from as early as I could remember. It was worthless, a trinket she bought at a store so many decades ago. To me it was priceless.

Sadly, it had gotten lost in the shuffle of belongings, and no one ever found it again. The transition from my grandmother blissfully dusting her many beloved treasures and carefully cleaning off the leaves of her jungle of plants to an empty house, disheveled and cold was startling. Those who knew her the best, her husband, her brother, and his sister, who was her best friend in high school, were the least interested in her lifetime collection of beautiful things. Only her daughter and I seemed to value them, and she got there first.

Strangely, though, the sudden evaporation of every childhood fantasy of this moment I'd ever had impacted me less dramatically than I expected. As a child I never really considered that my grandmother would die one day, but I knew she would be gone, and I would inherit her treasures. I believed I would live in my grandparent's house and care for their beautiful land that stretched all the way to the riverbank. I looked forward to growing old with my grandmother's beloved dogwood tree that I climbed into so I could enjoy the summer breeze during my lazy childhood adventures.

Now the home I loved was gone, every precious scrap of clothing and jewelry gone, and I quickly realized that even my familiar freedom to stand on the surviving deck my grandfather built by hand and gaze at the river would be gone. As those over seventy seem remarkably able to do, my grandmother's husband, a man who had become as dear to me as my own grandfather, quickly remarried. He and his new wife settled into the house, and she made it her own. I never went back.

The house was sold in 2016 to another older couple and has since traveled within their own family line and in the truest sense, I have nothing left from that time, except my memories and my trauma. But somehow, in the days and weeks after, leading all the way to the writing of this sentence, it has been a kind of freedom I never expected.

Losing the most precious person in my life did not devastate me as much as I feared when I was a child and imagined what that moment might feel like. I would find myself lost in a daydream seeing myself swaying alone on a built-in deck swing my grandmother and I loved to spend warm summer afternoons in. I fulfilled that prophesy, venturing out onto the deck, sitting in the decaying swing with its rusty chains and the worn-in scuff marks where we lazily pushed into the wood to gently move us in concert with the breeze. I finally knew what it was like and strangely, it was peaceful.

A month later I petitioned to change my name. I moved to a new apartment, changed my phone number, and prepared to graduate from college. I had fully embraced my new Jewish path and was on my way to full conversion. I was twenty-six and finally ready to start my life. One more life-changing event, however, was in store for me that would once again shake the foundation of my world.

After surviving hepatitis, I believed I had contracted a serious sexually transmitted disease and I was overly concerned with passing it on to someone else. So, my sexual activities came to a pretty dramatic pause. I still succumbed to the urges on occasion but was careful to protect my partner from exposure to me. It was so meaningless, however, that it became pointless to pursue and I considered the possibility that I had lived my sexually adventurous life, several if I was being honest.

But one evening in late summer, I decided to toss caution to the wind and take a chance with a compelling man I stumbled upon in a local chat room. He was only in town for the weekend, he was devastatingly handsome, and he was interested in me. I decided I would take him out to dinner that evening and then see where the night took us. I wanted to be romantic for once.

I arrived at his hotel room, so nervous and excited with anticipation I could barely stand still, when he opened the door, my excitement instantly turned to frightened confusion. Standing before me was not the remarkably handsome, professional man I had gazed at in awe on my computer, but a disheveled, zombified version of him instead. His eyes were deep and hollow, glazed over and vacant. His skin was spotted with small wounds that moved down his neck, indicating extensive meth abuse. His lips were dry and cracked and in a strained voice he told me to come in.

Still in shock I felt myself step forward, unsure of what to do next, and quickly found the door closed behind me. The next several minutes I only remember as an observer who was too afraid to watch closely. He grabbed me, overpowering me and began to pull off my clothes. I resisted, pushing him away, but at the same time feeling a sense of numb inevitability.

My next memory is the elevator door opening with a startling ding and walking by the same young woman at the front desk I had cheerfully greeted only fifteen minutes or so prior. She didn't look up. As I adjusted my clothes and smoothed my hair, I tried to hide my face, which I imagined was obvious and concerning. I went to my car as quickly as I could, got home, showered, and went to bed.

His voice haunted me, though, as memories began to trickle in. In one painful thrust he whispered in my ear, "You're mine now." In another he was babbling about giving me the gift of HIV. I couldn't piece the sequence together, but I realized one of the most tangible fears any gay man has had become a possibility. I went and got an HIV test.

A few months before, I had tested negative. It was my first test, and I had been talking with a man online who insisted I get one. I hadn't had any encounters between that time, I had been more focused on my grandmother. If it was negative, I told myself, I would never put my life at risk like that again. In an instant my entire future seemed to depend on the outcome of that test. I had lost all control and everything I worked for, fought for, seemed lost.

I had to wait for several days, the content of which I do not remember. I do, however, viscerally remember sitting in the patient room when the doctor came in and casually told me my test came back positive. I was engulfed in a cloud of buzzing devastation. The doctor was talking to me, telling me about what to do next, and so on, but all I could feel was a sense of deeply profound betrayal. In an instant my life seemed to end, and I had no path forward.

I managed to finish my last semester in school, get my degree and get my first full time job within a few months, but the experience was a blur to me. It was if someone else had simply taken control of my life as I fell into a void of nothingness. My life continued, even if I believed it couldn't possibly be done. For the first time, though, I had health insurance. The peace and certainty that brought worked to counterbalance the fear and shame.

I even discovered I never had hepatitis B at all, but tested positive for A. The previous diagnosis had simply been an error. Everything seemed new, but with a heavy awareness of the consequences only a cautionary tale can provide. But one part of my previous life remained in the back on my mind and my new access to a wide array of medical treatments brought it to the surface once again.

In 2008, my life started and seemingly ended at the same time. One unexpected consequence was that a long-discarded dream resurfaced as a new and realistic possibility. Remarkably, the company I began working for began offering transgender transition coverage for its employees. The primary barrier that had crushed my hopes years before was suddenly removed. The possibility of restarting that journey flooded my mind.

In my late twenties now, I laughed at how at eighteen I thought waiting until I was thirty to transition felt like a waste of my life. Now, as that milestone quickly approached, I realized it was the perfect timing. I could begin my therapy now, my father and grandmother were gone, and I had no one to judge me, I worked in a place where I could safely dress as a woman and not face discrimination or judgement, or harassment and I had insurance that would pay for the medical treatment and the surgery. It was everything I had hoped for, prayed for, desperately pleaded to the universe to provide me.

Yet now I wasn't so sure it was what I wanted. My old insecurities about passing came back and my body had become more masculine over time. I had a new name, a new religion, and a whole new life, and I wasn't so sure I was ready to take on another reboot. Now, I also faced the reality of being HIV positive and what that meant for not only medical transition but potential romantic and sexual partners. My ultimate goal was to find a heterosexual man to fall in love with me. If everything else went perfectly, my HIV status would surely be a deal breaker.

I remembered the words of those two transgender women I knew years before, and I carefully considered them. What was I really fighting to achieve? What would be different in my life as a woman that would make it better than what it currently was as a man? I couldn't answer those questions and I knew if I couldn't, a therapist would never approve me. Perhaps that was a good obstacle to be forced to overcome.

The true conundrum I was facing was that I loved the idea of being a woman, but I didn't mind so much being a man, as much of a man as I was. I had long given up trying to convince other men I was able to compete with them and I had grown to accept my role in my friend groups as the funny, flamboyant gay guy. Was it really worth the time, pain and risk?

Nine

More Than Surviving

At my new job, I discovered an entirely new group of peers and suddenly had value to add to the team. I had a chance at advancement and people seemed to accept me exactly as I was every day. I began to consider that maybe there wasn't really anything wrong with me to begin with. I still felt a great deal of pressure from other gay men to fit a more masculine-looking role, but I could still perform a one-man show of *Rent* without anyone blinking an eye.

At the same time, my understanding and appreciation of masculinity was beginning to change. I was becoming more active on social media, Twitter in particular, and quickly found that my perspective as a feminine gay man fit in well with the movement towards more acceptance of masculinity. I found the prospect appealing. Here was a group of men who embraced me exactly as I was and offered to teach me the secrets of masculinity, something I had longed for as an adolescent.

My history, my struggles, my conditioning, all of it fit into their worldview of a culture that was feminizing men and I was the perfect example of how to correct it. Maybe with the help of the very men I had fantasized about being accepted by would finally resolve the conflict. Could I accept myself as a man too?

As I crossed the threshold of 30, and surrounded myself with the world of masculine positivity, I found a tentative place of peace. Maybe the answer really was to become a superhero, as I imagined in my childhood. Lift weights, grow a beard, embrace logic and stoicism, reject modernity and feminist ideology, and finally fulfill my father's demand to simply be a man. For a while it seemed to work. I felt accepted, I felt much more confident, I saw my body as something to build rather than something to disguise or work in spite of, and I saw a path forward.

However, something wasn't quite right. Being welcomed into this new world, one I had been so cruelly barred from before, was exhilarating, but fleeting. I had to be careful about how I expressed myself and my natural impish and playful nature was frowned upon. I was struggling with my HIV regimen as well, facing side effects that caused me to gain weight, feel exhausted and lowered my sex drive. I discovered my testosterone levels were naturally dramatically low.

Testosterone supplements, exercising and hours of recreational feminist-bashing online did not seem to do much to improve my self-perception. I still looked in the mirror and felt a deep disconnect from my body. I gazed at women in public, with their stylish outfits and hair, perfecting the slightest deviation in their makeup with careful precision and I couldn't help but feel eight years old again watching my grandmother.

What embracing masculinity provided me in fulfilling my need for male companionship and approval, it suppressed in my desire for expression and creativity. Being a masculine gay man was much less fun than I imagined. I constantly felt the need to be in control of my body and its movements to such an extent it exhausted me. My voice was a constant issue as I became obsessed with every slight inflection and tone. Even the way I walked became a fixation that drove me to anxiety.

After boldly rejecting wholesale every aspect of gay culture that encouraged flamboyant behaviors, the men I talked with were as stiff and uncomfortable as I was. They always seemed terrified of being discovered as less than what they wanted others to see. I simply couldn't keep up with it all. I was tired and fighting so hard to craft such a precise persona had left me cynical and frustrated.

Masculinity is difficult to describe, but the most basic stereotypes seem to rely on a direct contrast to femininity. A man is the opposite of a woman in every way. A woman is emotional, and a man is in control of his feelings. A woman is impulsive and irrational, and a man is logical and level-headed. A man is strong, and a woman is weak.

Of course, this isn't true, but men have been validating their own sense of identity with these standards for a very long time and that influence has found a resurgence online. In the same way, those guiding the culture have long positioned masculinity as the source of all human woes, demanding that an empowered female-dominated world would finally save humanity from itself. I found myself trapped somewhere in the middle.

My grandmother was no feminist, but she wasn't a traditional housewife either. I once found an activist pin in her leftover belongings calling for passage of the Equal Rights Amendment, a movement specifically designed to include women in the Constitution.

She defied limitations and tossed expectations aside, proudly boasting of her many achievements in astonishing men in contests of masculine prowess. She preferred men, finding them to be easier to talk with and less intellectually tedious. She hated talking about domestic household issues, kids, fashion and so on. She wanted to talk politics and have a straightforward and vigorous debate.

Although she had female friends, she dedicated much of time participating in public activities men preferred. This was certainly relevant when she ran for office and became a lobbyist. She relished every opportunity to use her intelligence, dry wit, and devastating passive-aggressive attacks to knock the men she engaged with down a few notches.

She was very careful to teach me how to be a gentleman that respected women and valued their insight equally, however. She wanted to make sure the misogynistic instincts of her husband and my father wouldn't take hold in me. On the rare occasions I repeated a sexist joke I heard from one of them, she was quick to sternly correct me.

My father's idea of masculinity seemed to be of the very basic, rough and tumble, overly handsy, drinking with your buddies and driving fast cars variety that seemed both offensive and boring to me. I often thought of men as being unpredictable, violent, too easy to anger and far too easy to offend. Women were more reasonable and tolerant, in my experience, and you didn't have to be so careful around them.

From the black and white contrast of boys and girls of my childhood to the bullying obnoxiousness of my male peers in high school and college to the idealistic and nostalgic lamenting of the men in my men's rights and positive masculinity circles, I could never quite nail down what being a man actually meant.

It seemed to be something you either were or were not and it couldn't be learned or faked. Womanhood, on the other hand, seemed to be a far more expansive and open-ended journey that held very few limitations and rules. Being a woman was almost a choice, and one lots of women reveled in choosing. Being a man was an obligation.

Despite not knowing how to define the concept of masculinity for myself, I certainly knew it when I saw it. From my first sexual encounters onward, my attraction to men was explicitly an attraction to natural and authentic masculinity. Physically, intellectually, sexually, emotionally, all of it felt specific and easily identifiable, but impossible to impersonate.

I found myself repulsed by feminine men, annoyed by their mannerisms, voice inflections and overall presence in a room, despite my sharing all of the same characteristics. I held no interest whatsoever in men who looked like me. I pursued men who looked like, well, men.

While I found it frustrating to be discriminated against by gay men for my own lack of masculine characteristics, I was just as unforgiving in my own criteria. After once meeting up with a man a few years older, who towered over me by several inches, with a square jaw, deep-set eyes, and showed off an impressively muscular body, I quickly ended the date when he began talking and his higher pitched, gay sounding voice excitedly synced with the flamboyant flailing of his hands as he went on and on about a recent tanning experience.

I was seeking out an intangible quality I did not have myself but felt was absolutely necessary for any hopes of internal peace. I needed a man to take care of me, accept me, protect me, teach me and somehow in a way I could not explain, *be* something for me I desperately lacked since as far back as I could remember. Every man I met was a disappointment.

I was once challenged on my impossible standards by a friend who asked me a question I could not bring myself to answer, 'Why do you expect a man to be for you what you won't be for him?' Although he was referencing my selfish desire for his physical perfection in spite of my own laziness, in a way it struck me as a devastating truth I wasn't ready to accept.

Why did I expect a man to dedicate his time and energy to my insecurities over the very qualities I demanded he have for my benefit? What would he get in return? I reasoned I would be a perfect wife, if only I was a woman. But as a man, the relationship was clearly imbalanced and unsustainable. My own unhealthy obsessions with my body, my personality, my sexuality and so on were dominating every aspect of my life. It wasn't exactly fair of me to expect someone else to take on that burden for me.

Men and women seemed to have it so easy, from my point of view, and I often resented women who tossed away perfect specimens of masculinity over the pettiest of reasons. A man was simply a man, and a woman was a woman and together they complimented each other perfectly and I wanted that desperately, just not in the right order.

Masculinity seemed to be a natural and comfortable state for most straight men I knew or observed, only becoming a burden when others shamed them for their natural tendencies. Men seemed to just like being men, finding every possible opportunity to avoid nagging groups who followed them around complaining of everything they thought, said or did.

Women often seemed to resent men for their freedom and insisted they behave more like women. I always hoped I could provide a safe place for a man to not only be free to be himself but be appreciated for it. From those first comics, to movies and TV shows to lectures in school and college, I always felt a little bad for straight men who seemed to be shamed from every angle. I thought maybe I could save one.

It must be said that much of the discussion around what being a man, or a woman really is comes from the filter of those who do not understand or experience it themselves in the way most people do. Queer, feminist and trans activists insist on redefining these terms to better accommodate their inclusion.

Yet, objectively, the vast majority, more than 98 percent by current estimates of those aren't experiencing gender identity deviation, seem to understand precisely what being either is at an instinctive level, with very little interest in intervening to change it. Especially men.

It appears that the conflict comes solely from those like me who feel both a deep social obligation to meet the standards set by gender norms and dismantle them to spite the fact we never can. Rather than carve out a space for ourselves with the understanding that our experiences are inherently different, not necessarily wrong, but different, we seem obsessed with blaming happily normal people for being, well, normal.

As part of my own evolution, I began to realize this truth and rather than fixate on what I didn't or couldn't have, began considering what I already did. The world of normal human development didn't owe me anything and they weren't asking me to be anything more than I was. So what exactly was I fighting for, or against?

In 2017, I was enjoying a career, I had found a nice rhythm of exercise, I had stabilized my HIV regimen and I seemed to be on the path towards a nice stable future, if I could just find the right man to go along with me. By pure accident, I did, and it was certainly not the one I had anticipated.

A young man, thirteen years my junior, messaged me on Twitter to tell me he had purchased one of my books and was a big fan. Flattered, I responded and thanked him and thought he was cute but didn't think much more beyond that. He was persistent, however, and continued to message me with daily inquiries into my life. Soon I found myself looking forward to his messages, which became awkward and endearing video calls, which quickly turned into a nightly ritual.

I certainly never thought of myself dating a twenty-two-year-old as I had always chased after older men. But he charmed me with his broad smile and Scottish accent, and before I knew it, I found myself deeply caring for him. In an absolute moment of insanity, I found myself frantically driving a rental car to Baltimore to catch a flight to the UK where I planned to spend a single day with my him and meet his parents and family.

It all happened so fast it seemed predestined. I felt as though I wasn't making any decisions myself, just following the path before me with every step scripted and mapped out. It was as invigorating as it was unsettling but feeling Jacob in my arms for the first time at the airport terminal, it was all worth it. He would soon visit me as well in the US, we would get married and spend the next four years wading through the murky swamp of the immigration system together. But I had finally found another person on this planet who loved me.

Jacob arrived and every single barrier I had ever constructed collapsed instantaneously. He found me trapped deep inside and happily showed me the way out. He accepted me exactly as I was, and I found I couldn't access the barriers that I believed kept me safe for all these years when he was around. I had no choice but to be vulnerable and utterly myself.

This implicit vulnerability and my complete lack of ability to override it was distressing, despite the fact that I felt more at peace with myself than I ever had before. There was only one unforeseen obstacle that I discovered by accident that would come to redefine how I saw myself from that moment on. Despite twenty years of excessive, impulsive, reckless, and remarkably outrageous sex with complete strangers, in all manner of environments and form, I was completely unable to be intimate with my new husband.

The moment he touched me, my body would freeze, and I would go into a state of anxiety, numbness, and confusion. When we tried to be intimate, I would feel an overwhelming need to escape, and my mind would race with guilt, fear and frustration. After all this time, priding myself of all things on my sexual prowess, I was lost. I once again sought therapy, despite my reservations.

Something I had never expected before was the reality of trauma and my skillful ability to avoid addressing it. I always prided myself on my belief that unlike so many others, I never became an alcoholic, or a drug addict, nor did I ever become violent or abusive. I seemed to have very little impact at all from what I had experienced both as a child and from my sexual assault.

I was a functioning adult who had put himself through school, earned a degree and had worked my way up to a position I could be proud of. I had done everything I was told I would never be capable of doing. I didn't feel traumatized. I certainly didn't feel disabled. So why, at the happiest and most secure point in my life, would my brain suddenly break?

The answer came down to disassociation. The human brain, especially in children, has an amazing ability to distract from pain, fear, and other forms of trauma through fantasy, suppressing memories and disassociating itself from anything reminding it of said trauma. The expected behavior is that when a person feels safe, they lower their safety barriers and enjoy the experience they are having. My brain learned what sex was under trauma and associated it with being unsafe. Now that I was safe, it was protecting me from danger, which it interpreted to mean physical intimacy.

The disassociation also shed light onto why I found the fantasy of being a girl so much more appealing than the life I was living as a boy, one which was filled with uncertainty and fear. That fantasy became such a powerful escape that I couldn't imagine being happy unless I fulfilled it. Every time I faced a significant fear or stress in my life, my brain acted to protect me by pushing me into the primary fantasy I had held my entire life, if I was a girl this wouldn't be happening to me.

Simultaneously I got the unique opportunity to live out some of that fantasy, as I had when I pretended to be a girl online, through new technology that first transformed a photo of a person into the opposite sex and then augmented reality allowing masks and other artificial details to be added in real time to a face on camera.

The app, which circulated on Facebook like wildfire, took a photo of you and provided multiple alternate versions, including the opposite sex. The results were humorous and astonishingly realistic, as in my case, I had a sister to compare them to. Sure enough, the resulting photo looked almost exactly like her, and I got a glimpse into an alternate reality in which I had transitioned earlier in my life.

The first time I saw the imagine my chest tightened and I felt a wave of nausea and anxiety. I immediately held two conflicting thoughts in my head at the same time, realizing I might have had decent results after all and being grateful I never pursued that path. Having Jacob made this conflict less dramatic. Obviously, had I transitioned, I never would have met him, and he had been such a profoundly positive influence on my life, I couldn't imagine that reality.

That thought kept circulating through my mind. As I virtually transitioned more and more photos to recreate the experiment, I kept getting the same results. But had I gone through with it, what would my life, not just my face, look like at that moment? The firm reality of Jacob versus the intangible speculation of an alternate reality brought me new perspective. I was grateful for the glimpse into what could have been, but I was deeply grateful for what was.

The app, of course, couldn't tell if the photo was of a man or a woman, so a man could be transformed into an even more masculine version of himself as well. I performed the virtual transition on the same photos and was amused by the results of a much more masculine me, one with a square jaw, full beard, more prominent brow and deeper-set eyes. He was definitely handsome, but he wasn't me.

True epiphanies only come around once or twice in a lifetime and I certainly had more than my fair share, but this newest one was profound. Sure, I realized, with repeated failed attempts, that being masculine was not right for me, but perhaps neither was being feminine. At least not in the socially acceptable and stereotypical way we think of them. What if I was neither?

When I first saw the word 'non-binary,' I squinted my eyes and scoffed at such a concept. How could a person possibly be neither male nor female? Cutting a woman's hair short didn't erase her biology, and neither did putting lipstick on a man. Furthermore, interpreting this as "they/them" was even more absurd. 'They' refers to a person you don't have enough information to describe, but it doesn't work as a personal pronoun.

The concept, however, was intriguing. I was objectively male, but perhaps I didn't really fit into either set of gender norms, making me non, binary. But what exactly would that mean for my day-to-day life? It turns out, it wouldn't change a thing.

About the time I discovered the curiosity of transforming a photo of myself into the opposite sex, my sister introduced me to TikTok. I had seen ads for it, and it looked uninterestingly silly to me, but after showing me a few videos, I decided it was worth exploring. I downloaded the app and amused myself with the endless nonsense young people with cameras choose to share with the world, but I didn't really feel like I was in the right age group to participate myself.

Anyone who indulges this curiosity will tell you that this inhibition will soon pass and before you know it, you're ordering a circle light and hanging backdrops from the nearest blank wall. The real fun of TikTok is the ability to enjoy augmented reality with amusing face masks and effects, and one was that of a drag queen. The filter consisted of oversized red lips, dramatic eye makeup and huge burgundy curls that swayed with your head movements.

I tested out the filter and instantly found it deeply hilarious, but also strangely satisfying. From the eye rolling of my husband, I am absolutely certain that I looked ridiculous holding my phone a foot away from my face and recreating every RuPaul facial expression and body language movement I could muster. But the experience was intoxicating. Here was my face with drag makeup and my drag moves were on point. It was perfect.

I found I could perform to my heart's content, share it in public to an accepting and cheering audience and not actually have to risk rejection or embarrassment looking at my failed makeup attempts in the mirror so many years before. From the chest up, it looked like a real drag queen, and I had endless fun enjoying a feature of the app where a creator films part of a two-person skit or song and acting out the other part side-by-side. Soulful straight boys never knew what hit them.

Of course, I was not content to remain purely digital. I realized the endless possibilities in front of me for creative outlet, and I indulged every creative impulse I had. From sexy male crooning to boyband dancing to flirting with strangers in a virtual wig, it unleashed something in me that I loved. Of course, my husband was deeply embarrassed the whole time, but remained supportive.

I started ordering wigs online and then using makeup filters, I would lip sync along to my favorite songs, and many I had never heard of before, creating visually amusing, if not confusing 15 to 30 second videos. I kept my facial hair which added a layer of humor. But I was struck by how easily I transformed into a reasonably attractive woman and how convincing my body language was.

I channeled my grandmother into the person I began calling, Babette, and soon I had an entire catalogue of videos I happily shared online with friends, family, and my followers on Twitter, to great amusement and encouragement. As the technology improved, a new app called Reface emerged, allowing a person to upload a photo of themselves and be seamlessly added to the face of any celebrity they imagined. The app featured photos and short clips of popular scenes from movies, TV and music videos, allowing a person to see themselves realistically mimicking their favorite media moments.

I took to this very quickly, creating a library of memes of my face on the bodies of models and female celebrities, perfect for a surprise reply to a tweet. My followers loved it. My friends and family loved it. I finally found an outlet that seemed to work. Whatever dysphoria I had left vanished as I confidently posted photos and short clips of myself as a woman to my most prominent social media accounts and enjoyed the positive feedback flowing in.

Today this has grown into a bit of an online brand with me now producing a magazine called, *Oh, Honey*, with the cover featuring my bearded face blended into the head and body of various free-to-use fashion models. I've taken what was once the most private of my fears and deepest of my hopes and I've turned it into something I am proud to share with the world. And I didn't have to change a thing about myself to do it.

What have I learned about my own sense of gender? Mostly that practically, it doesn't influence my life nearly as much I believed it should. Certainly not to the point that I let it. Today I look inside, and I come out with my hands up indicating I have no idea what's in there. I don't know what my gender is, and I couldn't describe it if I tried. Rather than cause me distress, it has become something of a running joke for me.

I am obviously male, but I'm not really a man and I'm obviously not a woman. I'm sort of in between. Even then it's not clear if I am lacking one or the other or if neither really apply to me. Of course, I can only speculate on what either of those words means in terms of internal experience as I only know from watching others express what they think those words mean. We all rely on stereotypes and norms, yet there does appear to be a fairly universal standard for both sexes that I just don't conform to.

I don't really reject either set of norms either, I just don't experience them as being very relevant to me. This doesn't mean I hate sports and collect shoes; it goes deeper than that. But honestly, not by much. Gender is a complex and interactive algorithm of learned cultural behaviors that compliment natural instincts and impulses in the sexes. I may have naturally instinctive male motivations, I just never learned to express them in socially male ways.

As I enter my forties, I see my life now and I am content. Though the challenges of surviving trauma have only begun to rise from beneath the surface, my life is full of love, support, and purpose. Whatever it was I was looking for in a man, it no longer seems important. Whatever I thought I could accomplish as a woman seems like ancient history. There is nothing I would change that would prevent me from being exactly where I am today.

Truthfully, like pronouns, my gender only seems relevant and important to other people. Being a man is supposed to endow me with certain privileges and perspectives, as well as limits to my participation in public discourse. More accurately, looking like a man imposes these social requirements. I am constantly being lectured on what my experience must be like and what I must believe and think and feel because of this designation. Yet it's all meaningless to me.

I am, in the most literal sense of the word, just a person. I am a collection of experiences and I have a wide range of interests built on those experiences. But none of that is strictly, or even liberally, associated with being a man or a woman. I don't need to change the way I dress to be my authentic self and I don't need others to recognize my internal experience in order for it to be valid. In short, my gender doesn't really seem to matter.

What does this all mean for the argument of gender identity or gender dysphoria? I would say that my experience is an example, but certainly not a rule. I don't think it proves or disproves anything. I have absolutely no way of knowing what other people who experience gender confusion or dysphoria experience, just as I can't read the minds and hearts of those who have transitioned successfully and are happy with the outcome. I can only tell you what I know.

However, I would argue that my experience with gender is not particularly unique, and it is reasonable to question what exactly it is a child is experiencing when they express discomfort with their gender. I can't imagine that children, at least some of them, have a psychic awareness of their true nature and are able to articulate it confidently enough to base medical decisions on. I certainly don't think suspending my puberty with medical intervention would have changed the inevitable outcome.

The reality is, I just don't know. Like gazing into artificial photos of what I could have looked like as a girl, I am only speculating with what I know to be true. Had I gone through social transition, suspended my puberty and began hormone treatment as a young teenager, that would have been my only point of reference and I would have nothing to suggest my experience wasn't typical or positive. Whatever struggles I might have lived through as an adult post-transition, I would have no way of understanding in the way I imagine them now.

I can't tell you what would have happened if I had transitioned, but I can tell you what happened because I didn't. Regardless of the cause, I certainly experienced gender dysphoria as a child, my body was allowed to undergo normal puberty and I grew into a teenager and then into an adult. While the thoughts about becoming a woman, and the desire to do so, stayed with me, they dissipated over time as I moved farther and farther away from the strict social norms of childhood.

The extremes in my thinking, that I had to transform fully into a girl or somehow become a superhero, indicate to me that my perspective was wildly unrealistic. I was consumed with a solution that would, in my limited worldview, resolve the discomfort I was experiencing. There is no proof, however, that this would have been the case. All I knew was that I was suffering, and I was desperate to escape it and my black and white mind assumed the only way to do that was to become the exact opposite of what I was.

My escape was a fantasy, and I am not certain indulging that fantasy would have been beneficial, despite the temporary relief it might have provided. For example, when my mother let me play with a Barbie doll, she was giving me an outlet to explore something I had been forbidden from prior. The doll didn't hold any magical powers or profound social implications. It was simply a totem representing the very thing I thought would bring me peace that I was violently prevented from enjoying.

If my mother had bought me girl's clothing, grew out my hair, changed my name and pronouns and painted my room pink, it would not have helped me socially integrate at my new school. Splitting time between being a boy in public and a girl at home would have further deepened the confusion I was experiencing. Believing I was a girl while being so tangibly denied access to their world, including rejection and possibly violence from boys, would have been severely traumatizing.

Yet my father's relentless attempts at forcing me to interact with my male peers, without the buffering influence of any female presence, did little but exacerbate the dysphoria. The more time I spent with boys my age, the more profound the differences became. The other boys certainly didn't know their job was to be supportive teachers of the secrets of being a boy for my benefit. They resented my inclusion, and were extremely open in their rejection, regardless of what the adults in the room said.

I viscerally hated sports. I was not competitive, and I had no desire to play rough or exert myself so aggressively in front of other people. I hated being hot and I hated sweating and I hated running.

The games were too noisy, too confusing, too visually disorienting. For me, it was like being stuck in a tornado of activity with everyone angrily shouting for me to go in different directions. I lacked the basic communication skills boys possess to participate in team sports.

No amount of shaming, lecturing, or forcing me to participate changed any of that. It simply made me want to avoid it all even more. Whatever enjoyment I might have found in competitive sports as I grew older was deeply stained with the frightening and unpleasant experiences prior. It wasn't just me either, the other boys hated me being there too. I was forced and they were forced, and the rules required everyone to participate equally.

I made their experience worse by being there. My confused, frustrated, weak and unmotivated presence prevented them from enjoying the game they wanted to play to the highest level of competition they could reach. When I was alone with them, their frustration and anger was aimed at me, which only made the situation worse. They would inevitably get in trouble and their resentment grew. No one wanted me there and I agreed with them.

Had I been allowed to explore my own interests and creativity, I wouldn't necessarily have joined the girls in their activities, but I might have found more productive outlets in less competitive fields or areas where gender played no role. I don't know if being a girl would have changed that particular reality, but I do know that it wouldn't have been a requirement.

Finally, there was never truly an option to become a girl. I would have simply shown up to school one day in a dress, which I doubt would have made things much easier for me. The fantasy could be indulged by adults and very possibly embraced by other kids, but it would always remain a fantasy. There is no way to know how my body would have developed if natural processes were artificially interrupted, but I do know that in order to keep the physical changes that made me look like a girl would have required permanent medication and further medical intervention.

I believed I could become a girl if I just found the right solution. I didn't understand biology or the development of the body. Had my parents taken me to a doctor who promised they could make that dream a reality, imagine the psychological trauma that would have followed when I eventually learned that was never true. I could look like a girl, but I would never be female.

I had no foresight into what my adult life would be like. Prior to puberty I assumed it would involve a wife, a house, and children by the time I was twenty-five. I never could have predicted what my wants or needs would be ten years down the line, or even five years. All I knew was that I was in pain, and I wanted it to stop. I believed being a girl was the only way to do that. Imagine if adults I trusted and relied on had validated that belief for me.

As I grew up and my concerns adapted to the growing complexities of my life, my desires and needs surrounding my gender became less important. Perhaps this was just my own experience or perhaps, if left alone, is the natural progression from childhood gender dysphoria. Children who stop seeking therapy for this concern aren't studied. We simply don't know. But I argue that if it happened that way for me, there is a risk of it happening to other kids as well.

An adult has a much better chance of making a decision they can live with, and it is reasonable to argue only an adult can consent to such a drastic medical path. Even then, I remember the words of the transgender women who advised me, and I think if I had the means to do so at eighteen, I would have, and I can't imagine what the consequences would have been from there. Possibly good, but I know for certain the life I cherish now would not have been one of them.

Whatever the source of this pain, and it is a deep and lasting pain, the future is not set in stone for anyone. I shudder to think of what I might have done to my own body and there has been a profound sense of peace in accepting it just as it is on its own. In truth, the solution was not physical at all. I just had to step back and allow my dissatisfaction with my gender compare with everything else in my life and it turned out not to be a very high priority. The solution, ironically, cruelly, and profoundly turns out to have been to do nothing at all.

Epilogue

Tracing back through the memories of your life is a fascinating experience. I've dedicated much of my writing over the years to exploring how the past experiences of my life were relevant to other people and hopefully, beneficial to the reader. This challenge, to explore and understand how gender influenced my life, was unique.

It certainly didn't lead me where I thought I would go. When you look back to your childhood, you are effectively seeing the light from a distant star, a moment in time that doesn't exist any longer. It is filtered through your own memory, but also through the memories of those who witnessed with you.

As an adult, entering my forties and better appreciating the talks I have with my mother, sister and others who shared these experiences with me, I am continually amazed at how memory becomes a narrative rather than a recording of events. You have to take the pieces and put them together, cross referenced with the objective facts you know, and hope to come out with something both accurate and meaningful.

At the same time, memory does not exist as a singular moment or activity. Combined together, it tells not only the story of your life, but the framework that built who you are today. Not only do your memories tell you how you became you, but the memories of those in your lives influence that reality just as profoundly.

My mother was one of seven children, and her mother was, by all accounts, a cold and emotionally distant woman who resented the life stolen from her that her children represented. She was physically abusive to her children and seemed to enjoy the severe punishments she inflicted.

She, in turn, had been abandoned by her parents at a church and raised as an orphan, only to venture out on her own in her late teens, never knowing what a family could be. Her father was Native American, and she was labeled as a "half-breed," which significantly lowered her chances of finding a family. She faced racism and absurd bigotry as she reflected much of her father's physical traits.

My grandmother's father was the town drunk, who never held a job in his life and spent his evenings gambling what little money he came across while his wife and four children barely survived in an old log cabin with a dirt floor, he had won in a poker game. He came from a wealthy family that had direct connections to President Zachary Taylor.

He came from a family of pastors and while his brothers all took up the family honor and became pastors themselves, he aggressively rejected it all. He and my great-grandmother married when they were thirteen years old, and he left his home with his new wife and were homeless for many years. When he died, my grandmother was with him, along with her youngest brother, who had spent his life trying to save his father.

She told me of how moments before he died, he began to curse God for the miserable life he had lived and reportedly started screaming that he saw dark figures in the doorway where my grandmother stood. The demons took him away and my grandmother left, feeling a deep sense of relief she was never ashamed of expressing.

I know nothing about my grandfather's upbringing or his parents, but sometime after starring in his high school play and joining the Navy, dreaming of traveling the world, he became an angry, bitter drunk who took out his regrets on his son and blamed his wife for all his troubles. When he met my grandmother, she was barely sixteen, having lived on her own for nearly a year. He was nineteen and apparently asked her to marry him on their first date and she said yes.

His brother was a lifelong bachelor, the youngest of his siblings, who was shunned by everyone in his family except his protective older brother, my grandfather. He was known as a secret pervert and a homosexual but respected in the community as a leader.

My father and grandfather both confirmed he had been a leader of the local KKK and held meetings at the fire house, where my father and his high school friends were required to attend in order to be volunteers, something that was highly desirable in the small community. Very few black people lived in the area, and whenever a new family moved in, it was a local joke that they would unexpectedly have a house fire.

My great uncle also had a reputation for abusing young boys, frequently hosting drinking and pot parties at his house where he would put on porn and take advantage of the intoxicated young men, who were too ashamed to say anything or risk their position at the fire house.

My stepmother escaped her oppressively conservative and religious family to attend college in a different state where she met the father of two of her children, one she was pressured into killing through abortion. He left her during her second pregnancy, and she hid her daughter, sending her to live with her parents, so no one would know.

My father didn't even know she had a daughter until the day they signed their marriage papers and her mother showed up for the wedding with my little sister. She was tormented by isolation, being so far from her family and being with my father who resented her for weighing down his life. They had a son together.

She would become more and more obsessed with atoning for her abortion, which plagued her deeply, turning to church after church until she found the Pentecostal faith and devoted herself to it fully, much to the objection of my father who hated Christianity and blamed it for his lifetime of guilt and fear.

His uncle was a pastor, and my grandmother was determined to raise me to become one myself. Her grandfather had been a pastor as well. Her sister also became ordained but was shunned by her family for pursuing the path. She suffered from delusions, believing herself to be a prophet, had twelve husbands, two of which she married twice with husbands in between and her son committed suicide after struggling with his homosexuality at the age of twenty.

As fate weaved these lives together, their individual experiences, traumas, struggles, and dreams clashed with one another, bringing out the worst and most challenging aspects of each other. Cycle after cycle, as if each life was a repeat of the one before, weighed heavily over my head as I found myself part of that cycle.

Rather than understanding it all as a series of unfortunate events, or a curse, or evil inflicted onto us, when evaluating each story, each event, and consider its impact, it becomes easier to see a series of consequences instead. One domino falling onto another with each individual domino believing itself to be the one pushed, but never thinking of those who would fall ahead of them.

I don't know why I am gay, but there seems to be sufficient evidence to suggest bisexuality and homosexuality are simply a part of the human experience, being more or less prominent in different cultures at different times. All I know is that without any input from me, the tidal wave that is puberty crashed into me and my feelings towards men expressed themselves through autonomic systems and I reacted to what my brain and my body demanded of me.

My gender, however, isn't as clear. I don't think I was gifted with a unique, but temporary, psychic ability that allowed me to understand the true nature of my being as a young child, even before my memories began. But I do know that my insistence on being a girl was prominent very young.

My grandmother noticed my intense interest in her clothing and my feminine presence when I was two or three years old. When I came out, my aunt dismissively noted that anyone who had been around me since I could first talk wasn't surprised at all.

But was it my biology? Did something happen while I was developing inside my mother's womb? Did the stress she suffered impact me and perhaps even the anger and hatred her own mother experienced as she carried my mother in her womb?

I know my testosterone levels have always been low, below even the bottom number of the spectrum, but this doesn't seem to be true for every male who identifies as a female, regardless of their sexual orientation.

Through dozens of medical exams, psychological exams and family history discussions, it is apparent that I experienced severe anal trauma from some form of sexual violation when I was very young, between four and six. I still have scarring and other physical trauma to my lower intestines and colon. Believed to be the original source of my PTSD and my dissociative disorder, could this have created the split in my mind that made me believe I needed to be a girl?

One of my doctors believes so, arguing that my mind must have reasoned since my great uncle only interacted with boys, if I had been a girl, I never would have been victimized. The physical trauma indicates multiple, repeated abuse. Is that the cause?

Obviously, not all transgender people were sexually abused as young children, so perhaps my own disassociation created a unique form of gender dysphoria. Or perhaps all gender dysphoria is a form of delusion, disassociation, or other protective ways the brain attempts to reason itself out of frightening and stressful situations.

My dysphoria didn't end at my gender. I hated being so much taller and skinnier than the other kids and tried frantically to overeat so I could gain weight, only to become so dangerously anorexic in my teen years I was almost forcibly hospitalized.

I obsessed over my jawline being too narrow and slight, which traveled with me well into my 30's when I pursued surgical options to enhance it, which I could never afford. To this day I despise looking at myself in the mirror at side angles or seeing photos taken of me or video in which I turn my head, believing the lack of separation between my neck and my jawline to be deeply hideous.

I profoundly hated my genitals, from taping them between my legs as a young child, something my grandmother repeatedly tried to stop me from doing, to trying to hide any hint of a bulge in any outfit I wore in middle school, to obsessing over the size, shape, and appearance as a young adult, which were all under constant scrutiny from other gay men.

When I wanted to be muscular, I despised how my muscles never seemed to grow. When I finally gained weight, my anorexia returned, and I became fixated on being fat. When I lost weight again, I would stare at my stomach for hours in the mirror, trying desperately to find any hint of abs or other definition.

I have always been at war with my body, moving from one unhealthy obsession and delusion to another. Body Dysmorphic Disorder, (BDD) and Anorexia were not my only delusional conditions. Along with exaggerating the importance of various parts of my body and being unable to accurately see myself in the mirror, I suffered from other psychological disorders as well.

I went through a long period of severe delusion that my thoughts and feelings directly impacted the world around me, causing me to desperately obsess over my every thought, repeat phrases over and over to stave off disaster, draw protection symbols in my mind repeatedly and crumble into panic attacks and disabling anxiety when I felt my efforts were insufficient.

I believed I was intentionally being persecuted, had frequently cycles of hallucinations and amnesia, my personality shifted unpredictably. As a result of my early trauma, several psychologists have settled on the source of my amnesia, personality shifts, frequent changes in names and behavior and consistent episodes of disassociation as being Dissociative Identity Disorder (DID). A diagnosis that has caused me overwhelming shame and anxiety, despite being unable to deny the overwhelming evidence.

I long suffered with crippling anxiety and depression and after my HIV diagnosis, began to experience intermittent panic attacks, sending me to the emergency room dozens of times. After surviving an acute choking incident when I swallowed food and had to forcibly eject it, I lost the ability to swallow for several months, leaving me with an intense fear of choking on even the slightest amount of water.

All of these conditions felt involuntary to me, doctors and therapists explaining a series of symptoms that I was struggling to handle with names and proposed treatments. From my perspective, it all seemed to happen *to* me, as I became more and more determined to fight through it and live a normal, functional, and healthy life. Something I am still fighting for to this day.

I believe this book is about the consequences of survival and what trauma does to the human mind and spirit and how despite the worst of it, the spirit can be stronger and push through it. I feel this story illustrates the astonishingly complex world that surrounds a child, and how that world impacts their self-perception and sense of acceptance.

I argue that this book tells the story of a boy who believed being a girl would change his life forever, and never stopped dreaming or wishing for that reality. But in the end, the problem was never with him or his body or his ability or inability to fit in with his peers, but that he was never allowed to love himself. The only love he knew was painful and isolating.

However, I also take this opportunity to make the plea that the experience of gender does not have to be the devastating and desperate medical condition it is often presented as. It is only part of a person's identity, part of who they are, and the limitations it places onto them are artificial. I can't speak for everyone, or really, anyone, experiencing this themselves. But I know that I allowed it to take over more of my life than it should have.

I believe that regardless of how deep the pain and discomfort reaches inside a person, they can find all they need in what they already have. A person lifts weights or diets to change how their body looks and feels and if a person believes living as the other sex would make them happier, I support them. But I don't believe it is the only option we have to find peace and fulfillment.

I do, however, passionately advocate against early medical transition efforts in children. This I can speak to with confidence, regardless of the source of my dysphoria or how it compares to others who experience it. Children in pain will seek to stop that pain. They cannot understand its source or the consequences. They only want to stop hurting.

Of course, a child given the opportunity to indulge their fantasies with full approval and celebration of their parents, teachers, people on TV shows and the most important public figures in their world will happily take it. But what happens when that child takes off the dress, climbs into bed and realizes the fantasy isn't real?

The promises we make to gender dysphoric children, that they can live as a boy or a girl with new clothes, a new name, and a new room with new toys, showered with validation and praise, and that one day they will be that sex, is in of itself cruel. The child has no ability to imagine the physical requirements, restrictions and risks they will have to undergo once they begin to grow up.

They cannot possibly know what losing their ability to have a child will be like, or the limitations of physical intimacy they will be forced to live with as adults when they fall in love. They cannot understand the constant medical intervention, painful injections, surgeries, complications, and negative impacts to the rest of their body they will have to endure.

There is simply no way of knowing if their teenage self or their twenty-something or thirty-something self will look back with regret, anger, and resentment at what was done to them when they were too young and too trusting to consent. It is simply too big of a risk to be justifiable.

I hope that reading my story brings insight into what this experience truly is like. For those who may have never thought about how gender can intrude on one's life and leave a lasting scar that is difficult to hide, I hope this helps bring some understanding. I also hoped to illustrate that even under the most extreme of circumstances, as I recognize my own to be, a person can choose to be free and to have purpose. We are not doomed to repeat the pain our parents believed they were obligated to pass on.

I do believe that everyone who finds themselves staring into the mirror and desperately contemplating escape from their body, by any means necessary, is truly in pain. Wherever that pain comes from, it is real, and it is devastating. It's understandable why so many flock to transition as a profound change that will, hopefully, relieve it.

Medication helped relieve much of my anxiety and silenced the terror that is a panic attack. Therapy helped me understand the complexities of my mind and has provided a steady trickle of tools to manage it one step at a time. Having a strong and loving partner in Jacob who is patient has been lifesaving.

But for me, the most effective solution to gender dysphoria and all the pain, obsession, and hopelessness it brings, was to simply let it be. Fighting it only made it worse. Letting it happen, letting the thoughts and the insecurities and the frustration simply exist allowed me to live with it.

I pursued and earned my Masters, got married, adopted a wonderful dog, published nearly a dozen books, became a professional writer, started a small business and charity making quilts and reconnected with my mother and her side of the family. Healing is possible, its not just about survival.

I still find myself drifting off and fantasizing about being a woman. I frequently have dreams of being a woman, some where I have transitioned, some where I am only beginning to and others where I am merely impersonating one. I always wake up with a sense of validation and a slight sadness, but one that I recognizes does not restrict my option to be happy for the rest of the day.

Rather than fighting these moments or fearing what they might mean or that indulging them might unravel the life I am so content with living, I have found peace in letting them be a part of me. Whatever the cause or the solution, surrender and acceptance have been the most effective treatments I have found to date.

Accepting myself and looking back at the chain of events that forced me to become who I am today; I find purpose in sharing my experiences. I don't think I am anything special or unique or that I responded my life's circumstances in any heroic way. I was forced to live it and I was given the choice to let it define me or to define myself. I wasn't always successful or proud of my choices, but they were mine.

I think about the most impactful people in my life and the choices they made for themselves that created the circumstances I lived through, and I finally have a sense of understanding and sympathy. I can't speak on their behalf or defend how they responded to their own pain, but I can put it all into perspective. That perspective has been fundamental in my journey through not only gender dysphoria, but everything else that came with it.

Gender was my burden, and it was my escape. It gave me a way to live a new life inside myself and it made unreasonable demands of me. It followed me everywhere I went and defined how I viewed myself and the world around me. Freeing myself from gender liberated me. All of the parts of me, all the ways my brain tried to protect me and the consequences of the trauma I lived through no longer restrict me, even if they help in understanding who I am.

I chose to share the most graphic and disturbing experiences in my life within the context of gender because my gender played such a powerful role in those events and how I psychologically survived them. It is also striking how well my experience fits into the medical and sociological research conducted over decades that seems to provide an answer, just not one popular politics is willing to consider.

All I know for sure, and I can now say with profound confidence, is that being a boy or a girl, a man or a woman, or neither, wouldn't have changed a thing. I would never have escaped my life through the creation of an artificial one. Whatever causes gender dysphoria or contributes to the desperate sensation that a person is the wrong gender, I am not so sure transition is the answer.

I found my true voice when I stopped trying to suppress the voice I already had. I embraced my authentic self by letting go of the belief I wasn't good enough as I was. I discovered my body was never wrong or damaged or insufficient to allow me to live fully and to love honestly. Perhaps through the perspective of my life, others can view their own and find the same hope that I did. After everything, gender never mattered at all. I didn't have to change a thing.

Published Articles

I have been writing about my experiences with gender dysphoria and gender identity for popular conservative outlets since 2016. These articles shaped how I understood my own experience and how I shared that with others to highlight current events and controversial topics.

 I have included this selection of my work to provide a timeline of how my feelings evolved and to hopefully provide additional insight into the larger topic at hand. I've been grateful for the opportunity to explore this conversation with wonderful feedback and encouragement from my conservative friends and followers. Each article appears here as it was at publication.

If 'Transphobia' Exists, it is Entirely The LGBT Movement's Doing
October 29th, 2016
Huffington Post

I am reminded of the first time I really saw a transgender story in a movie. I came out in 1998 when I was 16 years old, and I devoured every part of gay media available to me at my local bookstore and Blockbuster. I rented a movie titled *Better Than Chocolate*, a 1999 Canadian film focused on the lives of two lesbians and managing their families. One character, Judy, was transgender. Judy was what everyone understood to be 'transgender' before 2015. She transitioned to a woman and attempted to live as one. Judy's storyline was of building a new life, reconnecting with her family and her crush on a lesbian character named Frances who was conflicted on the idea of dating someone who was not 'really' a woman.

It was about this time in my identity development I began exploring the idea that I too was transgender. I certain felt like I was female as a child and up until my focus became overwhelmed with my sexual orientation, I assumed as an adult I would somehow magically become a girl. Seeing Judy was curious to me. Judy was not the typical 'woman trapped in a man's body' stereotype in that she was also attracted to women. It had not occurred to me then that a heterosexual man would become a lesbian woman. Ironically it was the most progressive and activist lesbian character in the movie most uncomfortable with the new idea that a straight man could become her lesbian partner.

But the movie in many ways encapsulated the transgender experience. Judy was not an easy transition being visually masculine and struggling with her voice. At one particular moment of weakness she reverts to her deeper masculine voice. Judy was real. She embodied the emotional and physical reality of what transgender transition was like. She was dedicated even when nearly everyone she wished to receive love from struggled to get past that part of her. She wanted to be a woman, not a lesbian, not a trans woman, not an advocate. She simply wanted to be.

The movie ends with her parents buying her a brand new home. The gift is, unfortunately, also a goodbye letter stating they never want to see her again. Frances finally breaks through her wall and kisses Judy in an uncomfortable but passionate embrace. You cared about Judy and felt a sense of hope for her.

The movie, like most gay themed movies of that era, is focused on personal choices and empowerment. The characters have made a choice to live out their desires and develop a sense of who they are outside of the comfort and security of their families. There are consequences to this with some being good and others emotionally difficult. But in the end the character owns their choice fully. This is a message that inspires compassion, understanding and even support from most viewers. It humanizes the social narrative.

Today's gay left, sadly, has forgotten this message and has chosen the path of bullying scold rather than advocate for personal freedom. Zack Ford, former LGBT editor for *ThinkProgress* argued, "Was just sent a music video with a trans affirming message but a cis man playing a trans woman. I told them I wouldn't be sharing it."[57]

Today the LGBT movement consists of people who seem to define their entire sense of advocacy on complaining that people are not accepting them enough or appropriately. It isn't enough that transgender people are included in popular media and culture despite being only 0.3% of the population. The way transgender people are included must be carefully managed. When director Mark Ruffalo cast popular actor Matt Bomer as the transgender lead in his film *Anything*, the response to a mainstream actor/director making a mainstream movie involving a major transgender character staring a mainstream gay actor was: Outrage. Similar to the above quoted tweet, the anger was focused on the idea that a non-transgender person would be playing trans in a movie.

"There are many qualified trans actors and writers who could have played in and advised on the construction of the scenes you're about to edit into a motion picture. They will lose more work because of this," Mya Byrne, a trans musician and poet wrote on HuffPost. "We know you have good intentions. But those intentions have far-reaching after-effects that you, as cis men, don't experience."[58]

Actor Jamie Clayton, declared, "I really hope you both choose to do some actual good for the trans community one day."[59] Clayton plays Nomi on the hit Netflix original *Sense8*, a trans woman in a lesbian relationship. Her story on the show is almost identical to that of Judy's in that she struggles with her family accepting her new identity and the lesbian community's hot and cold receptiveness to her as a real woman. But the point here is that she plays a trans woman. Just like Laverne Cox does in *Orange is the New Black*. The characters are both interesting and unique and both provide a sympathetic look into this experience, but the reality is the actors themselves have limited their own potential. Ironically a decade ago it was viewed as progress and social acceptance for straight actors to play gay roles and vise versa.

How does bitterly scolding mainstream influential voices, one who is gay himself (Bomer), advance the pursuit of transgender acceptance? It seems this particular branch of the identity movement no longer cares. If the cult classic 1995 movie Jeffrey were to be made today the LGBT left would be chastising Patrick Stewart and Steven Weber for appropriating gay roles. Patrick Swayze, Wesley Snipes and John Leguizamo would be lectured on how one should hope they will do 'actual good' for the gay community one day after starring as drag queens in the film *To Wong Foo, Thanks for Everything!* Julie Newmar. If memory serves, Tom Hanks was not a gay man living with AIDS when he filmed Philadelphia.

The absurdity that actors must match their character's various identities in order to be authentic or 'good' for any particular community is beyond reason. Worse, the attitude itself limits creativity and shames artistic interpretation. They really should have cast a real sex worker in the movie Pretty Woman rather than a famous rich actress! It is nonsense. And yet it is the currently path the LGBT movement has chosen.

When challenged with a completely reasonable question by David Marcus, Senior Contributor to *The Federalist*, as to what empirical test could be used to determine if someone is a woman,

Ford responded simply with 'Asking.' Providing the current LGBT-led assumption that gender is determined solely by the person experiencing it. It is a reasonable question, yet the response is dismissal and shaming.

In another exchange between Marcus and Ford over the nature of 'woman' versus 'trans woman', detailed by Bre Payton of *The Federalist*, *Trans Activist: Using Pronouns That Align with Biology is Just Like Saying the N-Word,* Ford again dismisses the very idea that transgender ideology can be questioned at all. Instead he insists on a specific language, set of standards and understood principles before even engaging. Without submitting to those requirements he refuses to entertain anything said as other than inherently bigoted.

It is this attitude that I believe creates hostility between differing cultures of people within the same physical and social space. Before 2015 or so (before the bathroom wars began) transgender people were generally understood to be a part of the population. No one really gave it much thought. People didn't 'come out' as transgender, they simply lived as their chosen sex and moved on with their lives. The legal battles were largely won in the last century and it was possible to obtain a complete legal status change to reflect your new gender. As a society it seemed the transgender issue was settled.

But the left is never satisfied. It wasn't enough that adults could pursue gender reassignment if they wanted to. I, for example, explored it and decided it was not right for me. I affirmed my birth sex as my gender and built a comfortable sense of self around it. In previous times this would have been completely normal. A previous employer of mine even covered reassignment surgery and hormone treatment for transgender employees. I worked with a transitioning person here and there, saw them mid-way out and about and literally no one gave it a second thought.

But now the LGBT left has decided that transgender people are oppressed because companies do not hang signs saying 'If you feel you are a woman, please use the women's restroom!' and completely non-transitioned teenagers can't go into the locker room of their preferred gender. The things transgender people managed day-to-day for decades without concern or fuss are civil rights issues of the highest order today. Pronouns, once a polite part of society, are now weapons of intimidation and coercion. Children are being transitioned without their consent and parents are being told if their 5-year-old son tries on a princess costume they are morally required to begin hormone therapy.

Average people are relabeled 'Cisgendered' and tilt their heads in disbelief at the dozens and dozens of gender options primarily 20-somethings currently conjure up on a daily basis. All the while being accused of 'transphobia' and 'bigotry' for even questioning the validity of it all. In the 1980's parents worried their child might be gay and get AIDS (a legitimate concern). Today they fear their child will be convinced they are the other gender at school and they will be shamed as oppressive and hateful if they try to reason with them afterwards.

There will be a backlash as you can only badger people so long. In everyday life people roll their eyes and convey annoyance whenever the topic is brought up. People cringe at the uproar over Halloween costumes and most seem to think the bathroom issue is absolute nonsense. Most importantly, people do not want to care. If you asked most people they would shrug and say, 'I don't care what you do, I just don't want to hear about it every day.' But that isn't good enough for the left.

The right is concerned about freedom of choice. The left is concerned about accepting the new Utopian order. We don't care about adults making life choices, we just don't want ideology providing predators access to children, children being influenced into making permanent life-long decisions about their bodies or state and federal regulations demanding recognition of a radical new concept of human nature and biology imposed onto the masses. The left is concerned that somewhere someone used the wrong pronoun when speaking about a transgendered person and the federal government needs to intervene.

Resentment, annoyance and rebellion are natural responses to smug indignation. Call me a bigot long enough and I am going to start enjoying saying and doing things that cause you to flail madly around your room with your hair on fire. The left creates the cycle. They manufacture a crisis, repeat it with wild aggressive accusations of malicious intent, the population eventually gets tired of it and lashes back and then the left indignantly declares they were right all along.

Sadly for transgender people the road is not going to get any easier. Had the LGBT left not chosen to foist this manufactured nonsense onto the nation they would have continued living their lives in relative peace, facing only the shallowest of concerns. Now their sanity, validity, stability, reach of influence and respect for their choices are all up for grabs. By demanding that we are the ignorant ones unaware of science, the very foundation they base their identities on is closely examined and challenged. We never would have cared before.

People who would have never given a second thought to calling a trans woman 'she' now feel a sense of principle against being forced or shamed into doing so. Where people may have laughed it off before but never gone any further, now they feel a sense of satisfaction saying 'No, you are in fact crazy. Stop lecturing me.' And no one wants any of this to be imposed on kids. The move from 'Just let me live my life' to 'Why won't you affirm me?!' has turned imaginary opposition into genuine criticism of their worldview.

While I disagree that 'hatred' exists towards LGBT in general but transgendered people in particular, resentment and discomfort are certainly rising. As usual, social struggles always begin with the left. If transphobia exits today, it is entirely their doing.

It is harder to be transgender in 2016 than it was in 1999 because of the LGBT movement. This is why more voices and perspectives need to be heard. This is why reasonable gay people and rational liberals need to recognize why a centralized approved narrative for all things only creates turmoil and chaos. We used to persuade and now we intimidate and its the duty of everyone who wishes to live in true equality to stand up against the LGBT bullies.[60]

Gender Identity: Embracing My Masculinity
This article was originally published on the Huffington Post Blog but was removed for violating their rules of conduct
February 4th, 2017
Huffington Post

When I was a kid I wanted to be a girl. Some of my earliest memories are of me praying to G-d to change me into a girl when I woke up. I idolized my grandmother adopting her mannerisms and her personal style. She let me try on her rings and jewelry and I even got away with wearing her scarves. She painted my nails and even highlighted my hair, to test the color before using it herself.

I followed the girls around at school and would even invent elaborate games where I hid in order to play My Little Pony with them without getting caught by my teacher. I can remember a girl in my class who raised her hand in a particularly feminine way and I began mimicking her. She pulled me aside one day and told me 'You can be my friend without doing everything I do.'

My father simply did not know what to do. His dream was for me to fulfill the sports fantasizes he could never accomplish himself and he tried his absolute best to push me into participating. I could not have cared less. In baseball, I would always end up in right field spinning in circles or chasing butterflies around oblivious to the game happening around me. In basketball, I was unfortunately tall at an early age, but managed just enough incompetence to never be given any real responsibility on the court. I just run back and forth until it was time to go home.

I had long strawberry blonde hair that curled at the ends and my grandmother absolutely loved it. Once when facing the other way, a man called out 'Who is that little girl over there?' while pointing at me. My dad nearly punched the man in the face. It was agreed I could have a mullet in order to satisfy both parties. I was delicate, emotional, nervous and far too sensitive. Eventually the adults in my life realized no socialization was better than forcing me into group activities I hated and let me wander off along the river bank lost in my own imagination. I just didn't have friends until I reached the latter part of middle school. I didn't develop stable long term friendships at all until my mid-20's.

The irony of all of this is that throughout my childhood I utterly obsessed over masculinity. I loved comic books, X-Men and Superman being my favorite. I loved WWE wrestling. I loved watching bodybuilding competitions and looking through muscle magazines. I fantasized about superheroes appearing out of the sky, telling me I too had a superpower, and then rescuing me from a life that just did not seem to include me in it. I wanted giant muscular men to be my friends, protect me from bullies and help me become one of them.

The truth was I simply longed to be accepted by the other boys and I wanted to join in with them. I just had no idea how. I never learned how to communicate with boys. I would awkwardly stand quietly when forced to engage with them and they just looked at me like I was an alien. But deep down I only wanted to be one of them. I can remember reasoning, very early, that since I couldn't master the art of being a boy, perhaps being a girl would allow me access into their world. Boys liked girls. If I were a girl it would just be so much easier.

I carried that belief well into my 20's.

In my early 20's I explored the idea that I was transgender and spoke with several therapists about the topic. I watched documentaries, read books, studied online and I knew the steps needed to complete transition. I even had a plan for managing work while I transitioned. I bought women's clothing, a wig and some makeup and I tried very hard to pass for something that didn't resemble a drag queen at around 3am. I practiced my voice and my mannerisms. I told my friends and even my family. I was set. The only problem was money.

This was the early 2000's so transitioning in your early 20's was just not as common outside of bigger gay centers. Today I see young men in their late teens transitioned from the waist up living their day to day lives. So, at the time I realized I would just have to wait until I could afford to do it. Although this filled me with anxiety and frustration I accepted it as the cold reality I was faced with. But then something changed.

I was in college and by pure accident of scheduling, spent time with a guy my same age and his girlfriend who decided we were all going to be friends. He was sort of gruff and didn't talk much, but she and I got along great. Soon I was spending most evenings with them and more importantly, spending time with him without her there as a buffer. I always made sure to have a girl around when dealing with boys. Somehow, he and I bonded even though we had very little in common except his girlfriend and a general interest in video games.

Today he is one of my best friends. He became the first male connection I had that did not involve sex and he managed to teach me everything I had been longing to know since childhood.

I learned how boys talk. I learned how they banter. I learned how they jockey for position. He made fun of me endlessly and at first I absolutely broke down every time he did it when I was by myself. Somehow, I learned over time it was his way of bonding with me. To this day, he humiliates me multiple times when we hang out and I have learned how to punch back and laugh. He physically challenged me, taught me how to do things and even when he laughs that I am a girl to him, he always includes me.

Two years ago, I met another guy my age by pure chance who I would have been terrified to make eye contact with in high school. In fact, we went to high school together and he barely noticed me. He is older, extremely masculine and on the outside a guy you would never expect to be friends with someone like me. We met as he was dealing with a difficult relationship and I became his go-to for advice and encouragement. He taught me about loyalty and the bond men can have together in times of stress and difficulty. He never puts me down, he always encourages my best attributes, and he trusts me.

Between the friendships developed with these men I discovered my own masculinity and understood what being a man meant. The fantasy I developed as a kid involving superheroes made me believe real masculinity was out of my reach. What I realized was that once I removed everything I thought limited me, masculinity was all that was left behind. I am a man and it is my nature. Even if it isn't as pronounced or dominant as it is in other men. What I was trying to create for much of my life was an adaptation to my environment that was simply impossible. I never would have found the peace in connection to myself and in connection with other men had I transitioned into a legal woman.

This is controversial, but we as a society simply have not thought this through. Adults like me, encouraged by a subculture that celebrates the idea of transitioning into a new and better person, have convinced far too many that their early childhood experiences are absolute. I hear the stories of transgender people today and I know what they felt and I know what they were experiencing inside. The difference with me is that I now know why I felt it. I have discussed some of the absurdities of the medical and political world regarding gender identity today previously. I talked about the conflicting definitions and extremely vague concepts to which individuals define their whole lives. We begin transitioning children based on these ideas.

Had I been born a generation later I would have been dressed as a girl by age 9 and taking hormones or hormone blockers well into my teens. I would never have found the peace I know today because I would not only have continued struggling to create a new identity that functioned in society, I would have had an entire media industry behind me telling me I was a brave victimized minority doing so. The connections and self-awareness I am grateful for today never would have been realized.

Granted I cannot speak for everyone. But I can speak to what I see. Transgender individuals still suffer from anxiety, depression, disorientation and a never-ending battle for self regardless of where they live, how far they have transitioned or how accepting their environment is. I believe it is because they are trying a solution for the wrong problem.

We never give these individuals the chance to live in their bodies and understand themselves in relation to the rest of society. We tell them that in order to celebrate who they are, they must change everything about themselves. I would argue that I am a transgender success story. The mental anguish and confusion I experienced has been resolved without surgery or hormones. My gender aligns with my sex and all anxiety and unresolved emotional needs simply gone. Once I accepted myself as I am, I found peace I didn't know was even an option.

We live in a society that allows incredible freedom to customize one's life. I support that and would not hesitate in fighting for the continued freedom to do so. But we also live in a society that believes children validate adult problems and we are intolerant of the notion that children simply grow out of things. By default, we take away the choice of an individual when we allow their child-self to determine their adult-future.

The answer is not simple. It wasn't as simple as putting me in sports or sticking me in a room full of boys and walking away. But my father wasn't prepared for my struggle and had no other resources. My grandmother loved me, but encouraging my sense of gender confusion only made matters worse. From what I know now, if I had experienced more time with boys, older boys and men in situations where girls were not around to protect me I might have developed the necessary skills to survive. Bullying, as we call it, has a very valuable purpose in how boys engage with one another. If my weakness had been broken down I may have gotten back up stronger. As it was I had the option to hide and never challenged myself.

Boys need male-only environments, surrounded by men who appreciate the journey and won't interfere. Boys need to be taught, together, what being a man is like, what work is like, and what brotherhood and loyalty means. Boys need to exercise, play sports, compete, lift weights and understand what controlling and building their body feel like. Boys need to be challenged. Boys need to be separated from girls and taught that weakness is a choice that never benefits a man to own. Boys need to be free from the social experimentation of feminization. And I am sorry, but a girl dressed as a boy with short hair is never going to fit in and only makes things worse.

Much of our memories of being bullied as children are remembered through the irrational emotion of childhood. Yes, children are cruel, but the strongest people I know today fought back and learned what they were capable of as a result. The LGBT world is a neurotic over-sensitive mess today because our entire generation was told we should never have to feel anything but love and acceptance.

Acceptance is earned.

Masculinity is not toxic. It is not dangerous. It is not something that needs controlled or minimized or suppressed in boys. Masculinity is as vital as femininity and it must be embraced, cultured and celebrated. We cannot assume children know who they are or what they feel. We have to provide them with every tool available to develop a sense of self and then allow them to make their own choices when they are adults. Hopefully in the future more struggling young boys will come to the same realization I did before they lose everything trying to chase a fantasy. Embrace your masculinity and you will find peace.

To #ProtectTransKids We Must Address Child Exploitation and Sexual Abuse

*This article was originally published on the Huffington Post Blog but was removed for violating their rules of conduct and resulted in my contributor status being revoked.

February 23rd, 2017
Huffington Post

The LGBT media erupted in outrage today over President Trump's plan to override President Obama's sweeping transgender student guidelines specifically designed to ensure transgender students could utilize the bathroom of their choice based on their gender identity. The decision inspired the hashtag: #ProtectTransKids in which various lawmakers and The Human Rights Campaign urged voters to contact their representatives to express opposition.

The source of the outrage relies on the idea that transgender students face bullying and discrimination in schools, primarily regarding bathroom access, and the protections put in place are necessary. The problem, however, is that in light of recent media regarding the realities of sexual abuse of minors, it seems to me and many others that the outrage it misplaced. There are much more concerning issues threatening the safety and happiness of transgender minors than which bathroom they choose to use in school and it seems the LGBT left simply isn't acknowledging it.

George Takei became a topic of concern in the last day or so after video was released of him giving multiple interviews in which he romantically describes his first sexual experience at the age of 13 with an adult, aged 19. Mr. Takei did not hesitate or pause in providing remarkably vivid details of his encounter and in the interviews shown he, and his interviewers, reveled in said details. He never flinched, never seemed embarrassed, never for a moment considered the description inappropriate despite his widespread fame.

Janet Mock, my primary person of discussion here today, included in her book, *Redefining Realness*, discussion of her personal experiences as a sex worker in her young teens. Mrs. Mock is a transwoman, was interviewed by Oprah and is a celebrated transgender advocate. She participated in the recent Women's March as an adviser and has become a well-known voice for the transgender movement. In an essay titled My Experiences as a Young Trans Woman Engaged in Survival Sex Work, she discusses her entry in to the world of prostitution at age 15. Below contains excerpts with commentary on this essay.

> "I was 15 the first time I visited Merchant Street, what some would call "the stroll" for trans women involved in street-based sex work. At the time, I had just begun medically transitioning and it was where younger girls, like my friends and myself, would go to hang out, flirt and fool around with guys and socialize with older trans women, the legends of our community."

She began engaging in sex work directly, she states, at 16 in order to pay for what she refers to as her medical needs.

> "The majority of the women I idolized engaged in the sex trades at some time or another – some dabbled in video cam work and pornography, others chose street-based work and dancing at strip clubs (an option reserved for those most often perceived as cis). These women were the first trans women I met, and I quickly correlated trans womanhood and sex work."

She is firm in her stance that she holds no shame about her life as a sex worker arguing that it was her body and her choice. She states she perceived sex work as a 'rite of passage' for trans girls even though she originally judged the others. She goes on to describe the error of that judgement and the generalized stigma towards prostitution.

> "...I couldn't deny that witnessing the women of Merchant Street take their lives into their own hands, empowered me. Watching these women every weekend gathered in sisterhood and community, I learned firsthand about body autonomy, about resilience and agency, about learning to do for yourself in a world that is hostile about your existence."

Although I hold no judgement towards sex work as a concept, for adults, and in my libertarian views strongly believe in personal liberty in all ways that do not impact others in a harmful way, I am disturbed by many of the things she describes. I agree with her that is it her body and her choice how to engage, but she is telling this story from the perspective of a 15-year-old boy.

My biggest concern is the reality that these adult men, presenting as women in varying degrees, which she so fondly describes, knowingly allowed a 15-year-old boy to enter a world they knew for a fact was extremely dangerous. Not even discussing the issue of legality, as men they knew the realities of being a prostitute presenting as a woman and they not only did nothing to legally prevent her from engaging with them they did not even appear to have taken action to discourage her.

> "These women taught me that nothing was wrong with me or my body and that if I wanted they would show me the way, and it was this underground railroad of resources created by low-income, marginalized women, that enabled me when I was 16 to jump in a car with my first regular and choose a pathway to my survival and liberation."

Adult men mentored this young boy into a life that Mock herself describes as dangerous, "Sex workers are often dismissed, causing even the most liberal folk, to dehumanize, devalue and demean women who are engaged in the sex trades. This pervasive dehumanization of women in the sex trades leads many to ignore the silencing, brutality, policing, criminalization and violence sex workers face, even blaming them for being utterly damaged, promiscuous, and unworthy."

Yet she praises, idolizes these men and celebrates the time she spent with them engaging in this lifestyle. She goes on to say:

> "My hope is that being open about my experience as a teenage sex worker helps further conversations about how we can better serve folk engaged in sex work as a means of survival, and particularly vital to my community, how we can develop programs that create more appealing and viable options for young trans women, so sex work isn't their only option for support and survival. We need programs that help trans girls and women find affirming, affordable healthcare and

housing options, that shepherd them towards completing their education and that instills in them a sense of possibility."[61]

I do not fault her for her desire to provide more options for young people living her experience or wishing for a better future for them. But it disturbs me that she does not come out and state firmly that teenagers should not only refrain from engaging in sex work to begin with but never once denounces, lectures or even pleads with the adults in the situation to take action to prevent them from doing so. She seems to take for granted that sex work is inevitable if you are transgender and this includes if you are a teenager.

Mrs. Mock wrote this in 2014, but as recently as the Women's March of 2017 she wanted sex worker's rights and recongition to be included in the overall agenda, the march did not include her wishes to which she aggressively spoke out, in part by saying, "...her feminism rejects the notion that sex workers "need to be saved" or that they are "colluding with the patriarchy by 'selling their bodies.'"[62]

Transgender teenagers engaged in sex work do need to be saved. All minors in this situation do. As an advocate for transgender rights it utterly confounds me that such a loud and sought-after voice has yet to express this so basic of a concept. A common theme among all LGBT in discussing the realities of teenagers engaging in sex with adults, running away from home, becoming homeless, drug addiction, HIV rates and prostitution is the notion that they have no other choice.

They are rejected by their families and must find a way to survive. She herself inserts 'survival sex work' often as underscoring this idea. The problem is it in no way addresses the true nature of the problem. No amount of anti-bullying campaigns, school programs, hate crime laws, school guidelines, acceptance, affirmation or public praise is going to impact the reality that adults are standing by as children engage in dangerous activities they are often a part of.

It can be debated whether or not a teenager needs to transition to the point of becoming a sex worker to support the necessary supplies. But it should be an absolute standard by all that, as adults, it is our duty to make sure they never have the chance. Advocates in this position must call on all LGBT to recognize that it cannot simply be assumed or accepted that this is the norm and that we must work around it to support these kids.

Far too often liberal outreach involves making terrible situations more tolerable rather than utilizing resources to eliminate the threat altogether. Teenage prostitution should be a top legal enforcement effort across the country.

Unfortunately, major LGBT organizations seem content to chase bathroom laws and devoting resources to being outraged over cross-gender sports and whether or not girls can join the Boy Scouts. How are we fighting to 'keep trans kids safe' when we tirelessly focus on vague ideas of bullying while actively ignoring the reality of teenage sex work? How is the experience of a 15-year-old on the street selling his body less of a priority that a 15-year-old cross-dressing in school and being called the preferred pronoun?

We have a problem of accepting the sexualization of children often to the point of celebrating said experiences once we, ourselves, are adults. George Takei did a major disservice to all abused children by making it appear romantic, beautiful and something a child should cherish. Our stories matter and they should be told. It is why I have told my own story on many occasions. But it cannot be in the context of a larger social demand like 'affirmation' or 'LGBT rights.'

We must have the courage to stand up and tell the cold, brutal truth of our sexual experiences as children and teenagers with the sole purpose of bringing awareness and inspiring true action to prevent it from continuing to occur. LGBT as a movement must also have the courage to look beyond campaign slogans and 'protecting the message' and understand our vital role in this issue. We have for far too long seen the LGBT world publicly dismiss, deny and act offended that anyone would even ask the question while looking the other way at real-life prostitution, pornography and the active sexual experiences between teenage gays and adults.

We have a responsibility to stop it from happening if we see it, report it to the police, publicly shame adults who choose to endanger the lives of minors for temporary enjoyment and call out organizations that do not prioritize actual safety in favor of intangible concepts that look good in headlines. Our lawmakers do need to be aware of dangers facing transgender minors and it is honorable to demand we #ProtectTransKids, however it means nothing if we continue ignoring the exploitation of children in order to champion political ideals.

Transgender Suicides: What to Do About Them
July 27th, 2017
Public Discourse

I have personally experienced gender dysphoria, and I explored transition in my early twenties. I am aware of the emotional struggle, but I am also aware of the empowering realization that I alone control how I perceive the world.

In a recent discussion on Twitter, Chelsea Manning (formerly Bradley Manning), pardoned by President Obama after being convicted of espionage, argued that transgender "treatment" is necessary for the health of trans individuals, "because," Chelsea stated, "not getting medical attention for trans people is fatal."[63]

Manning's argument is anything but an isolated one. When seventeen-year-old Leelah Alcorn committed suicide in 2014, LGBT activists immediately jumped to blame his parents and society at large for causing the tragedy. Zack Ford of ThinkProgress wrote:

> *Leelah Alcorn's death was a preventable tragedy. Here was a 17-year-old girl with full access to all of the information available in the 21st century about transgender identities, including many safe and effective ways to transition. But as she wrote in her own suicide note before jumping in front of a tractor trailer this week, there was no hope attached to those possibilities — no trust that it could, in fact, get better. She had given up on crying for help.*[64]

This, despite the young man's parents support of his gender identity. He killed himself because his parents asked him to wait until he was eighteen to begin transitioning. They wouldn't agree to pay for it earlier.

The argument can be summarized as follows. Without medical treatment (expensive surgery and lifelong hormone therapy), social acceptance, correct pronoun use, and open bathroom access, trans people will never be comfortable in their bodies or in society. Consequently, they are at a high risk for suicide, and it's an injustice not to make these "treatments" available; the crime of killing trans people can even be laid at the feet of those who do not take these steps.

This argument, made by Manning, Ford, and so many others, is supposed to halt any criticism—or even querying—of gender theory, but it raises more questions than it answers.

If It Needs Treatment, Isn't It an Illness?

The various liberal resources are shockingly equivocal as to what gender identity actually is. Gender identity is an "innermost knowing," an issue of hormone imbalance, the result of a male brain in a female body, or a 'transsexual' brain, maybe an inherited characteristic, and many other possibilities, depending on whom you ask. According to some, gender is an inborn and permanent state; for others, a fluid awareness that might change by the day. How is it possible that a condition so insusceptible of consistent definition could be universally declared fatal without medical treatment?

Further, if transgenderism requires medical treatment, how can it form the basis of anyone's identity? Trans people and their allies have, of course, insisted with great indignation that their condition is not an illness, but it is hard to see how this conclusion is to be avoided, if it's insisted that it must be treated or else will be fatal.

Illnesses that require treatment do not constitute anyone's identity. Being HIV-positive requires medical treatment. I do not identify as HIV-positive as though it made me an entirely new kind of person. It is a condition I need to treat in order to live and be healthy. How is being trans any different?

Aiming at Sex-Gender Alignment

The goal of most transgender individuals is to live as the opposite sex. If this were not true, there would be no concern about "access to health care" or medical necessity. If one could simply enjoy whatever gender identity felt the most appropriate at any given time, medical intervention would be merely cosmetic. So if we agree that people who identify as transgender desire to be the opposite sex to the best of their ability—arguing that internally they already are—then we must accept that the ideal state for all individuals is cisgender, where gender and sex align naturally.

In my experience, this assertion is viewed as hateful and intolerant. To suggest that people who identify as transgender desire to be "like everyone else," "normal," or—dare I say—"healthy" by aligning their gender and sex is to suggest a transgender identity is itself a state of error. But again, this seems to be what is presupposed by the argument that medical intervention is so vital that, without it, a person may commit suicide.

In order to achieve a healthy and mentally stable state, a trans person must have their gender and sex as closely aligned as possible. Why, though, does this require the physical sex to change in order to align to the perceived gender? Why shouldn't the perceived gender be what changes?

It seems far more reasonable—and medically ethical and sound—to achieve this homeostasis by changing gender to match to the already established sex. A woman taking testosterone must continue taking testosterone, or else her desired masculine secondary sex characteristics will fade away (though if she has removed her ovaries, her body will not be able to produce estrogen and bring her female sex characteristics back). As many trans men prefer to keep their reproductive organs and become pregnant, this risk is even higher. The body's aggressive and persistent attempt to return to a state, despite medical interventions to override that state, indicates that the state is "natural." The body is being medically forced to adapt to conditions it is unsuited to experience.

If the ideal state is one of homeostasis, in which gender and sex are the same, then why would trans people dedicate their entire lives to forcing their bodies to adapt to conditions they cannot maintain on their own? It seems far more reasonable to recognize that the physical sex at birth is the standard by which internal perception should be aligned. Logically, wouldn't a transgender person who suffers due to misalignment of gender and sex be equally as happy aligning his gender to his sex if the end result is that gender and sex are the same? Why is the only acceptable option to force, through dramatic physical deformity, the body to adapt to the mind instead?

We Need a Real Cure

Some trans advocates would presumably reply that sex should change rather than gender because sex can change, whereas attempts to change one's gender usually end badly, but this response is unnecessarily pessimistic.

I have personally experienced gender dysphoria, and I explored transition in my early twenties. I am aware of the emotional struggle, and I am sympathetic to the sense of frustration and hopelessness. But I am also aware of the empowering realization that I alone control how I perceive the world. Even if I would prefer to be female, I understand that my body is male, and therefore the most effective and healthiest plan of action is to align my sense of gender to that unchangeable state. I have largely been successful, as I feel fully integrated today and am not only comfortable in my male body but find myself enjoying the pursuit of masculine physical progress.

An uncomfortable truth is that many surveys, including a 2011 Swedish study, indicate that suicide rates remain high after sex-reassignment surgery (the Swedish study reports that people who have had sex-reassignment surgery are 19 times more likely to die by suicide than is the general population);[65] and the National Center for Transgender Equality reported in 2015 that 40% of people who identify as transgender have attempted suicide.

The LGBT community actively fights such studies and suppresses the voices of people who, like myself, have chosen natural alignment or who regret transitioning. The medical community is currently uninterested in recognizing the inherent dangers and long-term impact of transition therapy and is equally unwilling to pursue study that may result in finding a cure or a resolution to the underlying issue. To suggest this is a medical issue needing to be cured is to be accused of proposing genocide.

But medical issues do need to be cured. If gender dysphoria is indeed naturally fatal without treatment, the only ethical solution is to find a cure that exposes the body to the least amount of risk. Obviously, this would be to correct the biological problem and/or address the psychological distress behind the dysphoria itself.

The LGBT movement has built a civilization around the validation of being "who you are" despite all efforts of judgment or persecution. Trans individuals often tell me they are now their "true gender." Advocates like Zack Ford and others routinely demand that extreme social bigotry prevents the trans individual from living a full and happy life. But in the center of this storm of indignation and boasting of perseverance is the steady and quiet realization that these people are extremely insecure.

We cannot forget the real tragedy in all of this. People suffering from genuine mental anguish are being promised that with enough surgery, camouflage, social acceptance, legal protection, educational campaigns, and so on, they will finally feel whole as a person. Worse, they are told that the only reason they continue to suffer is due to the intolerance and hatred of those around them. The current method of addressing this concern is only making matters worse. Treatment needs to address the core problem.[66]

I Was an Eight-Year-Old Drag Queen
October 18th, 2017
Public Discourse

Elle Magazine recently released a video of an eight-year-old drag queen who calls himself "Lactatia." The viral video features a young boy wearing dresses, wigs, and copious amounts of makeup. It praises his exuberant fascination with drag and his courage in choosing to live his life as a girl.

When I see this boy, I see myself. I see what could have happened to me if I had been born a decade or so later. And I wish I could warn him of the dangers that lie down that road.

My Grandma and Me

When I was eight years old, I too wanted to be a girl. I was utterly fascinated with all aspects of femininity. To me, my grandmother was the manifestation of femininity—stylish, sophisticated, and incredibly beautiful. She loved jewelry and makeup, and she never left the house in a less than perfect state of appearance. For nine years, my father and I lived next door to her, and she raised me. When I was eight, she was my entire world.

My father was in his early twenties when I was born. Divorce left him a single father, holding down two jobs as he tried his best to raise me. He struggled with my feminine impulses, always trying to push me toward sports and male friends and discouraging my grandmother's influence. But in the end, I don't think he knew quite what to do. I was depressed and lonely, and I had great difficulty connecting with other kids. Being around my grandmother made me happy.

I remember her testing hair dye on me by streaking my hair first to see how it would turn out. She always wanted me to be a little more blonde, but my red hair grew darker every year. She would paint my fingernails when she painted hers, only to remove the color before I went home at the end of the evening. We played with a doll house together and did endless crafts. She loved watching me run around her walk-in closet picking out the various accessories to her many colorful outfits.

I can remember fantasizing about what it would be like to wake up as a girl. I imagined it would make my grandmother happy, as she obviously wished I was a girl. I figured it would be easier to fit in at school, too. All of my friends were girls, and I was constantly being lectured by teachers to play with the boys. If I were like all the other girls in my class, maybe the boys would stop being so mean to me and finally accept me. It all just seemed to make sense to me.

Gender Dysphoria, Hyper-Masculinity, and Risky Sex

As I grew older, my feeling of being displaced in my body began to manifest itself in the opposite direction. I became obsessed with everything hyper-masculine I could find. I read comic books, subscribed to bodybuilding magazines, and watched sports, always trying to find some secret key to being a man. I wanted men to like me, and I figured these resources might be able to show me how to act in order to achieve that goal. I was always awkward and shy around other boys and men, and they would either ignore me or make fun of me.

As I moved into puberty, this fixation on the extremes of sexuality evolved into sexual arousal. I became sexually attracted to men, and I harbored a lingering longing to be female. As my obsession with masculinity grew into sexual fetishism, I became more and more adventurous, seeking out older boys to ask about this mysterious sexual world I only saw hinted at in magazines and on TV. This led to my engaging in sexual behavior with several male peers, all in their early teens. By age fourteen, I was hanging out in the basement bathroom at the library of the college campus where my father worked, engaging in anonymous sex with strangers. I experimented with drag and took on feminine sexual roles. My entire sense of self revolved around my sexuality and my sense of being "wrong" in my body.

My behavior grew more and more reckless. I even made plans with a stranger I met online who lived in California. He was supposed to rescue me from my small town on the day I graduated from high school. He actually flew into town to attend my graduation, and I discovered he had lied about his appearance, age, and practically everything else. The level of danger that I casually put myself into boggles my mind today. I am genuinely lucky not to have been killed.

All of this occurred in secret. I never spoke about my activities to anyone. Since my father trusted me to take care of myself, no one ever asked. My paranoia about others finding out, my embarrassment and shame over my sexual behavior, and my ongoing focus on radically changing my life the moment I had the chance left me anxious, extremely depressed, and disconnected from my family. It was only because a few significant life events forced me to stay put—my grandfather passed away a few days before my eighteenth birthday, and I moved in with my dad to care for him—that I was saved from running off, becoming homeless, a sex worker, or worse.

The Dangers of Sexualizing Children

I share this experience because it is absolutely vital to understand the impact that early sexualization has on children. The statistics are staggering.

Early sexual behavior increases the risk of sexual violence, both by young persons and against them. Young people between the ages of thirteen and twenty-four made up 22 percent of all new HIV cases in 2015. According to the CDC, "Studies conducted among teens have identified an association between substance use and sexual risk behaviors such as ever having sex, having multiple sex partners, not using a condom, and pregnancy before the age of 15."[67,68]

LGBT teens are also at risk of becoming homeless and becoming involved in prostitution. Unfortunately, some LGBT activists actually encourage this choice. Janet Mock, a trans woman and sex worker advocate who helped organize the Women's March in 2016, fondly remembers leaving school at fifteen years old and traveling to a known area of transgender sex workers to learn the trade. Praising the adult men portraying themselves as women for prostitution, Mock writes:

> *These women taught me that nothing was wrong with me or my body and that if I wanted they would show me the way, and it was this underground railroad of resources created by low-income, marginalized women, that enabled me when I was 16 to jump in a car with my first regular and choose a pathway to my survival and liberation.*[61]

As Mark Regnerus has pointed out, within the academy, some scholars are working to erase the taboo around adults having sex with minors.[69] This is clearly taking place on a broader cultural level as well. The first season of the TV show Queer as Folk featured a storyline in which a seventeen-year-old high school boy leaves his family to move in with a twenty-nine-year-old man he met at a gay bar. Similarly, a highly anticipated 2017 movie titled Call Me by Your Name portrays a sexual love story between a seventeen-year-old boy and a twenty-four–year-old man.

Meanwhile, children like "Lactatia" are being pushed to cross-dress in sexually provocative ways and to embrace a trans identity at younger and younger ages. National Geographic famously featured a nine-year-old boy dressed as a girl in 2016 as well.

It seems the Left has fully embraced the sexualization of children—with their parents' approval. We know what happens to young people who engage in these activities behind their parents' backs, but what happens when your mother actively encourages you? I fear this boy, fixated on a sexual persona and encouraged by media and activists, will never truly experience childhood. He will experiment with dangerous sexual activity at a young age. If he is exposed to drag culture in his very early teens, he will see drugs, alcohol, and anonymous sex as part of the culture he is told he belongs to.

Standing Up for Children

The Left celebrates its own sense of progressive insight and holds "Lactatia" up as a trophy of their enlightenment. But where will these activists be when he drops out of high school or becomes addicted to drugs? How will he ever know who he is when his identity is so wrapped up in the ideological agenda of a movement eager to exploit him for the sake of a political narrative?

Our culture has become so overwhelmed by the voices of sexual minorities that the average person feels helpless to speak up for fear of giving offense. As someone who belongs to that minority, I know it is absolutely necessary that you do speak up.

It didn't occur to anyone to ask me why I felt the way I did as a child. We must learn to notice depression or anxiety in children as an extreme warning sign—and then to act on it. Activists today would argue that had I been encouraged to be "myself," I wouldn't have experienced this level of depression. But that simply isn't true. My gender dysphoria was a symptom of a larger issue. Today, many want to turn psychological symptoms into an identity. In truth, what I needed was help understanding and overcoming my social anxiety. I needed tools to build healthy, lasting friendships. I needed exposure to masculine environments and strong male leaders. I needed to understand my own masculinity rather than fantasize about a feminine ideal.

Unfortunately, without a dramatic change in our culture, no child experiencing what I did will have that opportunity. We must stand up for them before it is too late.[70]

Why LGBT Activists Can't See What's Wrong With A 9-Year-Old Drag Queen
January 16th, 2018
The Federalist

Brandon Hilton, owner of an online clothing store specializing in erotic clothing, recently announced that nine-year-old drag queen Lactatia was his company's newest "cover girl." He tweeted, "I think this new generation of drag kids is brilliant and inspiring! @Desmond_Amazing and Lactatia are the future! @TheHouseofMann is just making sure they look SICKENING! People will talk no matter what, might as well give them something FIERCE to look at!"[71]

Hilton received an immediate and overwhelming backlash as people reacted angrily to the appearance of him sexualizing a child. He responded, "woke up to countless tweets telling me to 'kill yourself' and calling me a 'pedo' after we announced 9 year old drag superstar Lactatia as our new HOUSE OF MANN covergirl… if you can't handle a kid in a sequin onesie, maybe the future isn't for you."[72]

Hilton messaged me on Twitter after I challenged him to explain why he would encourage the sexualization of a child as an LGBT activist. Although his tweets seem to celebrate children engaging in these adult activities, he seemed profoundly disturbed by the accusations. He believed the outrage came from ignorance and hatred by "right-wing propaganda." While I think he did not intend to sexualize the child or promote pedophilia, I also think he cannot understand how his actions did just that.

Why Kids Are So Important to the LGBT Left

The images of the young boy are undeniably adult in nature, from the make-up to the posing, to the facial expressions. The boy is emulating an adult woman being sexually provocative. He has seen this behavior and body language in his drag queen mentors.

Drag is an inherently adult form of entertainment, meant to exaggerate female sexuality using humor and vulgarity. The sexuality within the artform cannot be separated out and therefore many oppose minors, and certainly children, participating in it.

Since LGBT people first celebrated the boy, he has been a symbol of a movement crossing a line. While those on the Right are quick to assert pedophilia as a motivation behind this movement, it is more rooted in sexual and gender theory that relies on children for validation.

Children expressing sexuality or gender identity that deviates from the norm are viewed as proof that this deviancy is inborn. And society is more likely to accommodate inborn traits than freely made adult choices. While LGBT Americans have full rights and are arguably widely celebrated in every sector, the LGBT Left has fixated on encouraging sexual expression in ever younger children. They genuinely believe they are helping these children by allowing them to "be themselves" in an environment free from judgment or repression.

The LGBT Left also believes denying one's "true self," which is often revealed in childhood, leads to homelessness, drug abuse, and suicide. They believe they are saving these children from a life of bullying, fear, and crippling anxiety. So any child who emulates LGBT culture is widely celebrated and promoted. A nine-year-old boy dressing and behaving as an adult drag queen is seen as beautiful and progressive.

An Identity Defined by Sexuality Struggles to Express Itself Differently

In June 2017, The Advocate, a major LGBT advocacy website and magazine, celebrated Lactacia.[73] The boy has become a celebrity in the LGBT world. Hilton believed he was promoting and celebrating a young boy he considers inspiring to his identity group.

The LGBT world often struggles to separate its sexually explicit culture from its advocacy for equality and rights. In many ways they are incapable of understanding why the outside world would be appalled by explicitly sexual public displays. For them it must be out of malice, hatred, or ignorance rather than reasonable aversion.

Gay pride parades have long been extreme public displays of every form of sexual deviancy imaginable. Gay liberals see no distinction between their sexual selves and their everyday selves. They celebrate the merger of the two as identity and culture.

The consequence here is that Hilton and the LGBT world will never be able to fully appreciate the damage being done to a generation of children pushed to grow up faster. The LGBT Left's intense focus on labeling then exploiting LGBT children holds incredible risk and threatens their futures. Early sexual activity and expression can be devastating to young people, especially LGBT youth. High rates of drug abuse, sexual abuse, and risky sexual behavior are common. HIV rates are extremely high for gay and bisexual young men aged 13 to 24. Nearly 40 percent of homeless youth identify as LGBT, with higher risks of drug use and sex work.

While the LGBT world may not be intentionally trying to harm children or put them at risk, it is time leaders of the movement fully recognize the dangers of using young children to validate their sexual politics. To help further this discussion, we must be careful not to abuse the term "pedophile." Overuse will diminish the impact of our message and make it more difficult to fight the legitimate scourge of child sexual abuse rampant around the world.

What we must do is call out the dangers of sexualizing children too early, making them vulnerable to people who do wish to exploit and abuse them. LGBT advocacy groups have a responsibility to recognize that every form of sexuality and gender identity can be freely enjoyed by adults in private, but should never involve children regardless of the context or motivation. While they intend to celebrate the uniqueness of the child, they in effect steal the child's innocence and impose an adult identity onto him, all to validate their own insecurities. We cannot stay quiet and allow more children to lose their childhood to the dreams of progressives who only imagine the future while failing to grasp the trauma they impose in the present.[74]

Here's Why I Choose Life Instead Of Ending It Like My Dad Did
June 12th, 2018
The Federalist

One of my first memories is of my father holding a bottle of pills in his hand, angrily sobbing, and ranting about how the world would be better without him. I was probably around seven years old then and my memory, as vivid and tangible today as it was in that moment, is of determination rather than fear or panic. I had done this before.

My grandmother told me my father would fall into deep and sometimes violent periods of depression as far back as a child, and often use suicide as an emotional weapon. She had grown to shake her head and simply walk away.

It took me far longer to understand or appreciate why. My memory ends with cleaning up the pills on the floor that he threw against the wall before collapsing into bed crying softly. I felt helpless, but also a strong sense of responsibility. I believed my job was to save him. I never really let go of that mission, until the day I had to.

I knew what he felt later, as I found myself in a similar place with a similar view of my own future. But my experience was a little different. I thought my life was over when I tested positive for HIV. I was in my mid-20s, in college, and completely on my own. I had a bright outlook on my future, dreaming of becoming a published author and political writer.

But the moment I walked out of the clinic holding that packet of information about my new illness, all of that changed. I sat in my car staring out at a future that looked very near and very frightening. I shared it all with my friends, but I still felt extraordinarily alone. In 2008, many doctors still described HIV as a terminal illness.

This Was a Severe Struggle for Me for Years

It took a little while and some courage to see a doctor and begin medication, because the weight of my depression and certainty of having no future made pursuing expensive medical treatment seem futile. But my friends persisted, so I began treatment. For a moment, my sense of hope began to bloom inside me again.

This feeling of possibility abruptly ended the first night I took the new wonder drug that was supposed to extend my life. I became sicker than I can easily describe, and the pain, migraines, and constant vomiting lasted four months. In an exceptionally weak moment one night, I stared at my greying face with bloodshot eyes streaming involuntary tears, and asked myself if it was worth it.

I made a choice that night that the rest of my life, however long I had left, was going to be mine alone and not dictated by the painful regimen of my medication cycle. My doctor had been clear when he waved away my complaints of side-effects, that if I stopped the medication I would die within a year. I decided to take that chance.

I sat the bottle of pills down on the sink that night and chose not to turn back. I accepted everything that was happening to me and realized I was helpless to fight it. In that acceptance, I found a sense of relief and purpose. I joked often that everyone wonders how he is going to die, and I was lucky enough to already know.

The depression never lifted and each cold, cough, or tired day sent warnings through my mind that my body was collapsing on me and the moment I had been expecting was there. So many times I fell into bed, softly crying and just waiting for the pain to stop and finally experience that moment I had become obsessed with finding.

In 2010, I wrote my book and fulfilled a dream I had almost given up on. The book was titled "Death Is Taking Me," from a joke my friends would often say whenever they felt sick. The book was part autobiography and part guide for others who found themselves in a similar place. My thesis was that there was no purpose in continuing to fight a disease through painful treatment when one could simply enjoy the remainder of his days as well as possible. I encouraged others to find purpose in their lives despite feeling profoundly unsure if I had achieved any in mine. Then I waited.

My Dad Kept Cycling Up and Down

Meanwhile, my father was beginning a new life. He married for the third time, and this one seemed to have promise. I had grown resentful towards him after delaying college until I was 21 because I felt an obligation to stay at home with him. I didn't think he could manage without me, and for the most part I was correct.

By age 23, I was still making us dinner every night and spending long hours talking about hope and continuing forward. But I had given up on watching him cycle continuously through these episodes of extreme hopelessness, only for me to endure stressful nights ready to call 911 at any moment and begging him to accept that he was loved. When he married, I moved out and thought that maybe my job was done.

Within a year he became extremely sick and we discovered he had suffered multiple small heart attacks. He required quadruple bypass surgery and the doctors were not confident he could survive it in his current health condition. He walked into the hospital expecting to die.

The night of his surgery, I stayed at home by the phone waiting because I could not bring myself to be in the hospital waiting for him to die. He thought I didn't go to the hospital because I didn't love him. But he did make it, and his recovery looked promising. For days after, a continuous flow of people visited to wish him well. I saw him genuinely happy and content for a very short time as he smiled and told me of all the people who had come to see him.

The peak of his joy took a sharp, sudden drop when the visitors stopped coming and he was ready to go home. He sat in his chair with his wife across from him and me on the floor watching a movie as he quietly wept. His wife and I took turns staying up all night to watch him.

On my last night with him, he was quiet and distant. So was I. But before I left to go home he looked at me, thanked me for staying with him, and told me he loved me. I told him I loved him too, although I felt it with frustration and anger. That night he overdosed on his medications. His wife told me he had insisted on getting his medications himself. She realized why too late, the next morning when she saw the bottles.

I Have Made a Different and Better Choice

My story ended differently. After years passed, my ambivalence towards my life grew less and less meaningful. I often joked I needed to write a new book titled "Maybe I Was Wrong." I didn't die, and hadn't gotten sick either. I had stayed distant from everyone and delayed so many things, then began to realize I had done so for nothing.

Who I am today comes far more from that moment of choice to try than all of the struggles leading up to it.

Then I got extremely sick with shingles, which nearly hospitalized me. My Jewish family insisted I see a new doctor. I did, and I was given the miracle of an unexpected sense of hope. I chose to try again.

That choice changed more than I had the capacity to realize then. My life today is something I did not think possible only five years ago. My husband, my writing, my career—all of it was never in the cards for me, as far I was concerned. I nearly allowed myself to miss out on all of it.

Today I have a manageable illness with a normal lifespan, and the choices I make affect my future once again. I have a purpose and a desire to live and experience as much as possible with my husband and the life we are building together. Suddenly decades seem paltry and far too fragile and limited. But who I am today comes far more from that moment of choice to try than all of the struggles leading up to it. It meant absolutely everything.

My father never truly got to know that sense of purpose or joy. With the burden of perspective, I better understand him now. I often wish he could have held on a little longer, and maybe we could have gotten here together. I wish he could see the life I have and that he could be a part of it.

Our separate journeys, however, demonstrate how powerful choice is to our lives. Love, friendship, and hope lift you up, but you must make the choice to grab on first. That is the hardest part for those of us reaching down to someone too lost in his own grief to look up. But for those of us lucky enough to be loved and encouraged, every single day gives us the opportunity to choose life. If my story has any message at all, it is that.[75]

The Atlantic's Article Should Foster A Consensus That Transgenderism Is Adults-Only
June 21st, 2018
The Federalist

The evolution of gender identity has outgrown the transgender movement, and conservatives and trans activists are struggling to keep up. Jesse Singal's article in The Atlantic titled, "When Children Say They're Trans," provides a powerful window into this reality, as does the reaction.

On the surface, many on the Right responded very well to the article, which details the struggles of many young people who began transitioning in their early teens and later changed their self-perception. In response, many on the Left, especially trans activists, responded with extreme outrage and hostility. As captured in a Twitter thread by a feminist account named 4thWaveNow, the immediate reaction to Singal's article involved an incredible amount of profanity and anger. One activist demanded that only trans people should tell trans stories, although the author presented trans individuals sharing their personal journeys. Well-known trans activist Riley J. Dennis referred to the article as "transphobic garbage."[76]

The article itself is exceptionally balanced and thoughtful, presenting difficult and very painful personal stories with care and respect. Singal is protective of his subjects and their stories and at no time indicates any form of malice or disapproval toward the trans community. In fact, while reading through each story one benefits from his gentle approach to describing and understanding core concepts within transgender theory. It is a remarkably beautiful piece. The problem, it seems, is that his work may have opened a door trans activists and the LGBT community would prefer stayed closed.

Critically, the piece is neutral, merely retelling the stories as his subjects see them. But their words give us insight into the experience of a young person struggling with who they are or who they may become. One subject, Claire who began this journey at age 12, tells us that after she discovered highly positive trans-affirmative videos on YouTube, she thought, "Maybe the reason I'm uncomfortable with my body is I'm supposed to be a guy." She just wanted to "stop feeling bad" and believed that once she introduced testosterone into her body she would feel better.

Claire's mother was supportive but cautious: "Most of the resources she found for parents of a gender-dysphoric child told her that if her daughter said she was trans, she was trans. If her daughter said she needed hormones, [Her mother's] responsibility was to help her get on hormones. The most important thing she could do was affirm her daughter, which [her parents] interpreted as meaning they should agree with her declarations that she was transgender. Even if they weren't so certain."

After Claire began living as a boy without medical intervention, she one day looked in the mirror and saw an intensely unhappy person looking back at her. "It was kind of sudden when I thought: You know, maybe this isn't the right answer—maybe it's something else," Claire told me. "But it took a while to actually set in that yes, I was definitely a girl." Other young girls in the article faced more serious consequences once testosterone was introduced into their system, like Max, who now has permanent male characteristics even after she changed her identity back to female.[77]

Trans activists have shown an intense intolerance towards those who initially felt they were transgender and then later changed their mind, including many who underwent physical transitions in the process. They often quote a very small percentage, 2.2 percent, of trans individuals regretting transition. But as Singal points out, this percentage is based on individuals who fully transitioned and legally changed their gender only to attempt to reverse the process.

According to Toronto Sexuality Center Director Dr. James Cantor, 12 studies ranging from 1972 to 2013 followed transgender individuals and collectively found that between 60 percent and 90 percent of trans adolescents ceased identifying as trans into adulthood. The truth is likely somewhere in between[78].

Because trans activists are so determined to dismiss and debunk the notion of people regretting their transition, even going so far as to call it a myth, it becomes difficult to fully understand the scope of the issue. Without hormone therapy or physical surgery, a young person who resolves their gender dysphoria on their own may never be counted. From the LGBT mindset, there is only one answer to this question and that is full and complete acceptance and affirmation of transgender identity. But their own self-regulating dogma has blinded them to the realities of the growing gender fluidity movement. By insisting that transgender therapy rely on medical intervention, the trans movement undermines its own evolution on what gender identity is.

In this, conservatives may also reevaluate our understanding of gender identity and sexuality. The gender movement is often absurd, and the hostility and aggressiveness turn us off to any persuasive arguments on their behalf. We have come to respond exclusively to transgender authoritarianism with, "There are only two genders." We do not separate gender and sex and recognize the biological reality of binary sex in our species. But in doing so we miss an opportunity to appreciate what the transgender community, at its core, is trying to tell us.

I understand gender dysphoria because I experienced it myself. As a young child and well into my late teens and early 20's I felt a distinct discomfort in my own body and certainly in my gender. I believed I was female and that transition would be the only way to experience peace in who I was. And while I have aligned my gender to my sex and am comfortable as a male, I cannot easily articulate what "feeling like a boy" means. In truth, I can only imagine what other men must feel like based on social cues, entertainment and observation, but I can never be sure. In the same way, as a child I could only imagine what feeling like a girl was like based on those same criteria.

Sex is biological, and we have two sexes. But gender is not so easy to define and for some, impossible to understand for themselves. What we are seeing today is a movement of endless possibility and self-customization online that fuels creativity in young people who suffer from insecurity and long for a strong identity.

Transgenderism as it has traditionally been applied requires a strict gender binary in which one is either male or female. It assumes that the intellectual and emotional experience of gender is firm and based exclusively on physical characteristics. Singal's brilliant discussion helps illustrate this perfectly. While trans activists may view his piece as an attack on the validity of what being transgender means, he is more accurately validating their experience through contrast. By limiting themselves to binary physical characteristics, the trans movement shackles itself to a gender worldview they so desperately want to break free from.

The trans movement has resorted to responding to such insight with accusations of ignorance and bigotry, but their intolerance demonstrates their greatest insecurity. The existence of individuals who ceased being transgender should not threaten them or their worldview, and there should be room for evaluating the methodology regarding beginning transition in childhood based on potentially temporary feelings. These stories matter, and it does nothing but harm the transgender movement to dismiss them with hostility.

From the conservative side of the argument, I think it is important for us to recognize that gender identity is something that has become a part of our social consciousness and the individual desire for uniqueness is not going to dissipate. Rejecting wholesale, the idea that gender can be confusing and difficult to define will only exclude our voice from the conversation. We have a unique opportunity to genuinely protect the future of many children by recognizing their struggle with compassion, while working to prevent overzealous adults from permanently scarring them, both physically and emotionally.

Singal's extensive review of the current state should be read and appreciated as it provides us an important insight into what is happening to so many children in our society. We have largely remained outside the argument, merely commenting with appalled dismissal. But a generation of young people is facing permanent physical scarring, sterilization, and emotional abuse based on a singular and powerful political voice.

Ideally, we would not care how adults choose to express themselves and if they chose to transition it would be their choice alone. But we must find a balanced and agreed upon way to allow children and adolescents searching for their identity to do so safely. Gender dysphoria will only increase, and the conservative movement needs an answer that is both compassionate and rational.

The stories of those, like myself, who were drawn to find resolution in personal insecurity and social isolation from our peers are an important window into how our society understands gender. Those who followed the transgender path, trusted the experts and medical authorities, and hoped their experience would mirror the glamorized images they saw online, only to still feel lost, should be heard. The aggressive and loud objection from trans activists should be rejected in kind. Transgender transition must be an adult decision and children must be able to find who they are without social coercion to change everything about themselves.[79]

My Rape Doesn't Justify Punishing People Without Due Process
September 19th, 2018
The Federalist

I walked past the same people at the front desk who had given me directions to the room where I had been raped shortly before. I was disheveled, my eyes were red from crying, and my clothes barely fit correctly as I rushed to rearrange them in the elevator to appear as normal as possible.

I was in a building filled with people, and my only thought was to get out as quickly as I could before anyone noticed me. I made eye contact with the girl at the front desk, who tilted her head slightly as I rushed by. I felt an instant wave of shame and fear. I even worried she might call the police, thinking I was a prostitute or perhaps someone on drugs.

I walked down the long sidewalk. It was late evening by then, and I was in more physical pain than I realized from the adrenaline pushing me out of the building. I slowed my walk for a moment, feeling a breeze, and I took in a deep, frustrated and embarrassed breath.

This was not supposed to happen to me. I was careful, I thought. I was a man. I was a gay man, and being assaulted in such a way wasn't supposed to happen to us. I felt deeply ashamed, and in all the times I had rolled my eyes at characters in movies not immediately calling for help, I felt genuinely sick at my cowardice. But I kept walking. I had parked a few blocks away, and made it to my car safely anonymous.

I don't remember going home, showering, or looking in the mirror that night. I don't remember going to bed that night or thinking about what had just happened to me. I only remember looking at my computer screen at the open chat message showing the rapist's cheerful excitement about my impending departure. I exited out, shut down my computer, and resolved never to look at it again.

The first person I told was also one of the first people I told I was HIV-positive. This person was the only one who asked how it had happened, and I let the story flood out in tears while gasping for air. The whole time I begged my confidante with my voice to understand that I did not want to be someone who had been raped.

My attacker was intoxicated, and possibly on drugs, as I remember his glassy eyes that seemed to look through me completely. Holding me down with his forearm on my neck, he told me he was infecting me with HIV. I still remember the aggressive passion in his voice that told me how much it excited him to say so.

I didn't have to escape. Once he was finished, he behaved as though we had just enjoyed a fun time together. He sat down on a chair looking at me with pride and amusement. I remember feeling like I chose to leave and therefore hadn't really been raped.

Maybe I was being too sensitive. Maybe I was being too prudish. Maybe I just didn't understand what was supposed to happen in this kind of situation. I had met a complete stranger in a hotel room, after all. It was my fault.

I was no stranger to unwanted sexual encounters or situations in which I felt out of control. I had been with men I did not enjoy and had just waited for it all to be over before. This time was just more violent, painful, and extremely paralyzing. It was my fault for freezing. I must have given him reason to believe this was what I wanted, and I couldn't deny him just because I had a momentary fear of what was happening. I felt like a fraud even suggesting the encounter was what other people describe as "rape."

I was in denial for a long time. It took more effort to allow myself to accept that label than to accept what happened to me or the lifelong consequences that resulted. Ten years later, I still remember the terrifying feeling when someone said, "You were raped," and what it meant to who I was as a person.

As might be apparent, I did not report the crime. By the time I found the courage to even verbalize what had happened, before I even accepted what it was, it was too late.

I beat myself up over and over, going through all of the things I did wrong that night that could have put that monster in jail. If I had just walked up to that front desk and asked them to call the police, they could have arrested him, gotten his DNA, and maybe convicted him. I could have gotten in my car and gone to the emergency room and told them, allowing them to do all the things experts know of in a safe place where people would have protected me.

I could have said or done something. But the more time passed, the more I realized my ability to prove what happened had faded into nothing, and I was terrified of the risk of reporting and being viewed with skepticism or outright judgment.

From TV, college classes, awareness campaigns, and so on, I believed the police would assume I was lying or had been doing something illegal, or simply dismiss me altogether. Besides, didn't I agree to meet him? Didn't I go to his room and walk in? Could I argue that there was no opportunity for me to fight my way out? Why didn't I say anything while leaving the building?

While replaying the scene over and over, it felt less and less believable to someone from the outside. The question hanging in front of me that I feared most was, "Why didn't you do anything to stop him?"

There is a good and valid reason sexual assault advocates so strongly fight questions about why a woman would not report her assault, wait so long, or not do anything to stop it. But there is also the recognition that, once a certain amount of time has passed and certain evidence is lost forever, there is no justice to be had.

This is a cold and objective truth that we too often overlook because of how unfair it is. Accusing a person requires proof, and the only time proof is available is immediately after the assault. After that, it becomes harder and harder to prove your story and, as the accuser, it is your responsibility to do so. To protect victims, too many advocates forget the importance of due process for everyone, equally.

There is also a moral and ethical obligation with recognizing what happened to you and the power you wield from your ability to accuse. If I stumbled upon the man who raped me, as I have often thought about, could I accuse him in public? Could I shout his name and the crime he committed against me that has redefined my concept of intimacy, autonomy, and lifelong health?

The answer is no, because I cannot prove beyond a reasonable doubt that the man in front of me would be guilty of the crime I'd accuse him of, and he would be utterly defenseless to my accusation. I do not have the right to name a person, turn his life upside down, and ruin his reputation. It's not because I am not entitled to justice but because I am simply unable to prove an assumed innocent man is guilty.

Survivors should be listened to. Our stories matter, and I have tried with more energy than I thought possible to share mine for the good of others, awareness, and honest debate. But I draw the line at accusation. My window to accuse closed before I even had the awareness to know it was an option, but that is reality.
It's not because I am not entitled to justice but because I am simply unable to prove an assumed innocent man is guilty.

Regardless of how unfair and unjust it is to the person who survived, the person accused has an equal right to a fair and just trial. Accusation requires proof, and that proof must be scrutinized and evaluated. The truth is, I do not remember key details of this event, such as the date or what I was wearing, or even exactly what my attacker looked like. I remember his voice, the way he smelled of alcohol, the grip of his hand, but I do not remember his name or even his username. Memory is not perfect, and therefore it cannot be solely used as evidence.

I cannot tell you if a person's account of his or her assault is valid or not. I cannot tell you to believe all survivors. But I can tell you that there is a difference between sharing your story and naming a person in an accusation. The longer a person waits to do so, the more scrutiny and skepticism is warranted.

Their story can, however, exist as a powerful tool of empathy, experience, and survival without exploiting the natural outrage people feel when discovering a villain they can target. The power of survival is using your voice to help other people survive and hopefully prevent the sense of helplessness you once felt.

But I do not believe we have immunity to accuse without consequence, and as a survivor I advocate due process and the concept of "innocent until proven guilty" more now than ever. Don't blame a person for not reporting sooner, but don't damn the accused to compensate for it.[80]

Even Though I Feel Non-Binary, Identifying As My Biological Sex Makes Sense. Here's Why

February 7th, 2019

The Federalist

The LGBT term "non-binary" has been popping up lately, from Vox's tribute to women and non-binary photographers, to states like Washington allowing a third gender option (X) for birth certificates and driver's licenses. The Washington law defines the "X" gender designation as, "A gender that is not exclusively male or female, including, but not limited to, intersex, agender, amalgagender, androgynous, bigender, demigender, female-to-male, genderfluid, genderqueer, male-to-female, neutrois, nonbinary, pangender, third sex, transgender, transsexual, Two Spirit, and unspecified."

The most common and widely used definition of "non-binary" is "genderqueer," which indicates the full spectrum of people who do not identify as either male nor female—people who identify as some blending of both or people with other concepts of alternative gender.

What Do All These Terms Mean?

Truthfully, the differences between the stated categories are minimal. For example, agender, androgynous, neutrois, and nonbinary all describe the same sensation of having no gender, when compared to male and female. Amalgagender, bigender, demigender, genderfuid, pangender, third sex, and Two Spirit indicate some blending of the two sexes to one degree or another.

The other options indicate a transition from one gender to the other, although modern transgender messaging insists that none of the above listed options are finite or reliably defined. It comes down to the individual and his or her own preferences at any given time. While members of the LGBT community argue these classifications of human gender and sexuality are separate, distinct, and natural conditions of humanity, the reality is they are simply detailing what has always been understood as individuality. Not all people experience all things in the same way.

As someone with direct experience in this introspective analysis, I believe these distinctions are fairly irrelevant to normal, everyday life. It is puzzling to me to see the concept as dramatically expressed as it is by LGBT media and advocacy. Gender conformity matters more in childhood than it does in adulthood as it seems, regardless of the efforts of the adults around them, children self-segregate into male and female peer groups.

This was particularly challenging for me as a child, because I identified with my female classmates more closely than my male classmates. I was daily aware how unlike the other boys I was was. Left on my own, I played with the girls, talked with the teachers, and gravitated towards the girls' toy selection. My favorite colors were pink and yellow, and I drew princesses and flowers constantly.

My perception was always that girls had easier and more enjoyable social experiences, and male behavior expectations were tedious and absurd to me. I simply did not understand why everyone wanted me to change my behavior—everything from the way I talked to my body language to my personal interests—to be more like the boys, whom I viewed as idiot barbarians.

I did not understand the social hierarchy or interactions in the male world, from my own peer group to teenagers to adult male gatherings. Leave me with a group of middle-aged women, however, and I was right at home. I found female dress, makeup, hair, and jewelry fascinating, and I thought I was a girl trapped in a boy's body well into my late teens and early twenties.

Despite All This, I Know I'm Male

Masculinity always felt like a set of skills I needed to learn but could never really understand. I fixated on masculine behaviors and attempted to mimic them, but it always felt like acting. On the other side of the spectrum, my attempts to dress as a woman, change my voice, or imagine a female version of my name felt equally fabricated and forced. When left alone, I was more or less, well, non-binary.

In all honesty, I cannot articulate what it means to feel like either a man or a woman. I can list gender stereotypes I have learned from media and observation. I can go into great detail about the differences in psychology and behavior I have studied in both sexes my entire life. But I simply cannot tell you what either feels like personally. It's all mimicry and acting to me. When I am "myself," I do not feel a sense of gender at all, and find that the perception of masculinity or femininity depends on who I am around.

The point of this observation is to illustrate what those on the trans spectrum articulate to one degree or another and to humanize the experience. For me, strict gender stereotyping is unnatural. I have absolutely no idea if most people understand that concept, but from my interactions, I have concluded that most people seem to have a pretty clear idea of what male or female means to them. It is equally possible that those who transition experience just as strong a personal knowing as the majority of the population. I can only speak to my own perceptions. But I can objectively tell you I am male.

I know I am a male because of my anatomy and regardless of how I have felt about my body, my social interactions, or my personal sense of self, I am a human male. There are people born with bodily anomalies that make this distinction legitimately difficult, and it is true that not every person has either XX or XY chromosomes.

But the objective reality is that the vast majority of people are either male or female and feel unquestionably as one or the other. This really brings me to my point on the relevancy of gender identity in the abstract. Regardless of how I have felt over time or my internal sense today, the fact remains that my body is male and that is the sex I should abide by in terms of legal classification and interactions with sex-segregated situations. Why? Because it simply makes sense.

My health indicators are male. If I experience a heart attack, I will have the symptoms of a male. Even if I pump myself full of estrogen and testosterone blockers, my body will forever attempt to reestablish itself as male. To this end, the concept of a third sex for identification purposes is irrational. It is also completely ineffective.

What possible point would there be for me to put "X" on my driver's license when my sex is not controversial to the casual observer? Even if I dressed in stereotypical female clothing, it would not alter my physical anatomy. The fact that I do not experience a specific gender in no way affects my sexual orientation, either. In truth, my sense of gender does not affect anything in my life outside of an awareness of not fitting in with conventional sex-segregated social activities.

Outward Gender Expression

I choose to wear male clothing because I look ridiculous in female clothing. It really is as simple as that. In truth, the most common outward expression of genderqueer individuals seems to be adopting stereotypical aspects of the opposite sex. In our culture, this is a perfectly acceptable option. It just is not one I choose.

I advocate for adults who do choose to express themselves using the full palette of style, fashion, and accessories in any way they like. But I find it unnecessarily confrontational to demand specialized protections, designations, laws, or mandatory pronouns in order to do so. Our culture of self-obsession has made an interesting quirk about a person far more burdensome than it should be. Growing up is hard for everyone, but as an adult you get to be whomever you choose. We should celebrate that rather than complain that not everyone acknowledges it in the precise way we wish.

I think the biggest shift in mindset for me came when things like how I personally experienced gender were no longer priorities. Building a career, battling through a serious illness, and starting my life with a new person changed my perspective on introspection. Spend enough time in your own head, and you'll find a remarkable number of things to fixate worry on. It's when you live outside of yourself and experience life with others that these things lose their importance.

I think that is the difference between being genderqueer and having gender dysphoria. One allows you to explore how you wish to express yourself, while the other becomes an unhealthy obsession that limits your ability to function without intervention. Much of the LGBT community is sadly pushing self-exploration into unhealthy obsession.

I also have lost the need to be validated for my gender as either a man or a woman. I recognized that most men think I am feminine, and most women think I am perfect. I like who I am, and I gave up trying to be somebody else.

The left will continue to designate ever more slight differences in experience and perception under labels they demand require special treatment and protections. But in the end, it is simply the progressive way of attempting to understand individuality. For most of us, the categories are truly meaningless in everyday life.[81]

How Ryan Anderson's Banned Book, 'When Harry Became Sally,' Helped Me With Gender Dysphoria
March 1st, 2021
The Federalist

In July 2017, I took a risk and submitted an article to a publication that I respected and read frequently, hoping to provide conservatives a perspective they may not have viewed before. I wanted to address why suicide was so high among transgender people and ask questions about transition I hadn't seen asked by mainstream LGBT sources.

I wanted to present my voice as a person who experienced gender dysphoria, pursued transition, then later found myself grateful I didn't go through with it. So with nervousness, I sent the article to Public Discourse, the online journal of the Witherspoon Institute.

I'd hoped for a positive reply, but I didn't expect a response from Ryan T. Anderson, a conservative voice I had respected for a long time. He thanked me for sending my story. Ryan took a risk on me, an amateur writer, and offered me my first professional writing opportunity. He also published another personal story about my experience with gender dysphoria. Throughout both interactions, he was kind, generous with feedback and recommendations, and interested in what I had to say.

When his breakthrough book, "When Harry Became Sally: Responding to the Transgender Moment," was published, I excitedly downloaded it to my vast Audible library. To say his book was eye-opening is to provide a vague description. I had not heard the arguments he made before, nor read through the scientific research and other objective examinations of the condition and its effects the way Anderson presented it before. I also had not heard stories of other people who had gone through what I had until then.

I Thought I Was the Only One

I rarely discussed my gender dysphoria because I never transitioned, and I assumed something was unusual about me. I connected emotionally with most transgender stories right up until they began medical intervention and then I felt out of place and truly alone.

In many ways, I saw myself as a failure because the only transgender stories I encountered were those who accomplished what felt impossible for me. I was embarrassed to even bring up the topic because I didn't want to have to answer the humiliating questions about why I stayed trapped in the "wrong" body all these years, or admit something inside me kept me from moving forward.

Anderson shared deep, rich stories by people just like me who did transition and then realized it was a mistake. Then they faced rebuilding the body and the identity they socially and medically altered in pursuit of some intangible goal of idealized gender.

Their understanding of discomfort in their bodies resonated loudly with me, even more than the initial concept of being transgender. I saw my struggle in their accomplishments, and I realized how truly grateful I was to have hesitated earlier in my life. When I wrote my story and sent it to Public Discourse, I thought it was unique because I hadn't seen it before. I didn't know I was among many friends.

I soon realized Ryan's work offered me so much more than just a sense of personal validation in my journey. He also offered me answers. The book goes in-depth into the science behind biological sex and what we understand about the human body and how it functions.

Anderson moves through the development of a human fetus into brain development and what science tells us can affect that development. He answers the question, to the best of his ability and using the most pertinent science available, why the argument in favor of gender identity over biology is flawed.

The arguments he makes are positioned within the compassionate and empathetic interest of a scientist trying to understand what is causing a person so much pain and what can truly be done to relieve it. Without ever dismissing the experience of the transgender person, he asks the important question, one I struggled with for years, of whether a medical transition is genuinely the best option to alleviate gender dysphoria and all the pain and suffering associated with it. He bravely challenges the arguments supporting pro-transgender therapy in children and imbues the reader with the information necessary to understand why.

The Left Is on a Book-banning Crusade

For years I have championed this book to those interested in fully understanding the transgender movement, its arguments, and how to challenge them on the science, especially regarding public policy. When I saw that Amazon had removed Anderson's book without so much as leaving the listing, complete with its history of valuable commentary from other readers, my heart sank. When I found out that LGBT activists were cheering on the decision, I sighed with frustrated disappointment.

Anderson's "When Harry Became Sally: Responding to the Transgender Moment," is not an anti-LGBT or anti-transgender work. Ryan is not anti-LGBT, and he was never dismissive or cruel to transgender people. His work is certainly a far cry from anything resembling "hate speech."

Like Abigail Shrier's, "Irreversible Damage: The Transgender Craze Seducing Our Daughters" and Dr. Debra Soh's, "The End of Gender: Debunking the Myths About Sex and Identity in Our Society," also targeted by LGBT activists for banning, Anderson's book asks necessary questions that deserve to be given fair consideration and debated, not restricted from public view.

For people like me who may have gone years feeling alone and completely ignored by the popular discussion of gender identity, Ryan's book gives us hope and understanding of ourselves and the options we have for our future.

That, in its simplest form, is the best argument for keeping this book and others like it available for people to consider and decide for themselves how to respond. Instead, LGBT activists seem to feel entitled to decide what information we should have access to so that we only make the choices they believe are best for us.

We live in an era of absolute human potential and knowledge. We have access to information and ideas beyond anything most people who ever lived could have dreamed possible, yet we find ourselves restricted by powerful, ideological Puritans who believe this freedom is dangerous. I hope that Amazon corrects this mistake before it causes further damage to the free ability to decide for yourself what you want to believe.[82]

Appendix

Figure 1: Occurrence of trauma (<4 vs. ≥4) for GD patients and controls.

	Controls (n = 123)	GD patients (n = 95)
<4	114 (93%)	42 (44%)
	(sr = 2.8)	(sr = −3.2)
≥4	9 (7%)	53 (56%)
	(sr = −4.4)	(sr = 5.0)

<4 = individuals with experiences of fewer than four typologies of trauma; ≥4 = individuals with experiences of four or more typologies of trauma (polyvictimisation).

Figure 2: Comparison of our GD sample and literature data frequency of trauma.

		GD (n = 95)	Clinical sample* (n = 56)	t (df = 149)	Effect size (Cohen's d)	p	FDR
Neglect	Mothers	1.50 (0.65)	2.03 (0.66)	−4.766	0.81	<0.001	0.000
	Fathers	2.12 (0.32)	2.07 (0.76)	0.364	–	n.s.	n.s.
Reject	Mothers	1.33 (0.48)	1.75 (0.62)	−4.366	0.80	<0.001	0.000
	Fathers	1.65 (0.85)	1.64 (0.56)	0.059	–	n.s.	n.s.
Role reversal	Mothers	1.30 (0.42)	1.39 (0.62)	−0.990	–	n.s.	n.s.
	Fathers	1.05 (0.18)	1.12 (0.34)	−1.428	–	n.s.	n.s.
Psychological abuse	Mothers	1.11 (0.16)	1.22 (0.24)	−3.087	0.57	<0.05	0.015
	Fathers	1.15 (0.22)	1.18 (0.21)	−0.758	–	n.s.	n.s.
Physical abuse	Mothers	1.16 (0.29)	1.39 (0.54)	−2.979	0.57	<0.05	0.016
	Fathers	1.24 (0.40)	1.32 (0.49)	−1.063	–	n.s.	n.s.
Sexual Abuse	Mothers	1.02 (0.13)	1.04 (0.18)	−0.851	–	n.s.	n.s.
	Fathers	1.01 (0.06)	1.03 (0.15)	−1.165	–	n.s.	n.s.
	Other figures	1.09 (0.29)	1.06 (0.22)	0.564	–	n.s.	n.s.
Domestic violence	Mothers	1.21 (0.48)	1.46 (0.62)	−2.586	0.47	<0.05	0.021
	Fathers	1.27 (0.59)	1.46 (0.62)	−1.862	–	n.s.	n.s.
Separations	Mothers	1.20 (0.58)	1.29 (0.62)	−0.814	–	n.s.	n.s.
	Fathers	1.56 (0.90)	1.75 (0.89)	−1.243	–	n.s.	n.s.

Figure 3: Adult attachment interview (AAI) classifications distribution (secure vs. insecure and organized vs. disorganized) for GD patients and controls.

	Controls (n = 123)	GD patients (n = 95)
Secure (F)	75 (61%)	26 (27%)
	(sr = 2.4)	(sr = −2.7)
Insecure (Ds, E, U, CC)	48 (39%)	69 (73%)
	(sr = −2.2)	(sr = 2.5)
Organized (F, Ds, E)	107 (87%)	51 (54%)
	(sr = 1.9)	(sr = −2.2)
Disorganized (U, CC)	16 (13%)	44 (46%)
	(sr = −3.1)	(sr = 3.5)

F, free/autonomous; Ds, dismissing; E, entangled/preoccupied; U, unresolved/disorganized; CC, cannot classify; sr, standardized residuals.

228 • SURVIVING GENDER

Figure 4: Sex differences in brain structure and function across the lifespan among presumed cisgender individuals

Male

In utero
- Testosterone and its aromatization to estrogen cause masculinization of the fetal brain

Adolescence
- More between-network connectivity
- Larger grey matter volume
- Lower grey matter density

Adulthood
- More total brain volume
- More grey matter volume
- More white matter volume
- More cerebrospinal fluid volume
- Higher proportion of white matter
- Larger volume of the central subdivision of the bed nucleus stria terminalis
- Better visuospatial and mathematical ability
- Weaker right-hand preference

Female

In utero
- Absence of androgen production and estrogen-binding activity of alpha-fetoprotein cause feminization of the fetal brain

Adolescence
- More within-network connectivity
- Less grey matter volume
- Higher grey matter density

Adulthood
- Less total brain volume
- Less grey matter volume
- Less white matter volume
- Less cerebrospinal fluid volume
- Higher proportion of grey matter
- Thicker cortex
- Higher global cerebral blood flow
- Better perceptual speed and fine manual dexterity
- Stronger right-hand preference

Notes

1. American Psychological Association (2015) "Guidelines for psychological practice with transgender and gender nonconforming people." *American Psychologist*, 70(9), pp. 832–864.
2. Prestigiacomo, Amanda (2016) "5 Times 'Transgender' Men Abused Women And Children In Bathrooms | The Daily Wire." *The Daily Wire*. [online] Available from: https://www.dailywire.com/news/5-times-transgender-men-abused-women-and-children-amanda-prestigiacomo (Accessed 30 June 2022)
3. Wood, Melody (2016) "6 Men Who Disguised Themselves as Women to Access Bathrooms." *The Daily Signal*. [online] Available from: https://www.dailysignal.com/2016/06/03/6-examples-highlight-serious-problems-with-obamas-bathroom-rule/ (Accessed 30 June 2022)
4. Greene, Chad Felix (2017) "Transgender Suicides: What to Do About Them - Public Discourse." *Public Discourse*. [online] Available from: https://www.thepublicdiscourse.com/2017/07/19769/ (Accessed 27 June 2022)
5. Olson, Kristina R., Durwood, Lily, Horton, Rachel, Gallagher, Natalie M. and Devor, Aaron (2022) "Gender Identity 5 Years After Social Transition." *Pediatrics*.
6. Ghorayshi, Azeen (2022) "Few Transgender Children Change Their Minds After 5 Years, Study Finds - The New York Times." *The New York TImes*. [online] Available from: https://www.nytimes.com/2022/05/04/health/transgender-children-identity.html (Accessed 27 June 2022)
7. Giovanardi, Guido, Vitelli, Roberto, Vergano, Carola Maggiora, Fortunato, Alexandro, et al. (2018) "Attachment patterns and complex trauma in a sample of adults diagnosed with gender dysphoria." *Frontiers in Psychology*, 9(FEB), p. 60.
8. Devor, Holly (1994) "Transsexualism, dissociation, and child abuse: An initial discussion based on nonclinical data." *Journal of Psychology and Human Sexuality*, 6(3), pp. 49–72.
9. Maggiora Vergano, Carola, Lauriola, Marco and Speranza, Anna M. (2015) "The Complex Trauma Questionnaire (ComplexTQ): development and preliminary psychometric properties of an instrument for measuring early relational trauma." *Frontiers in Psychology*, 6.
10. Nuttbrock, Larry A., Bockting, Walter O., Hwahng, Sel, Rosenblum, Andrew, et al. (2009) "Gender identity affirmation among male-to-female transgender persons: a life course analysis across types of relationships and cultural/lifestyle factors." *Sexual and Relationship Therapy*, 24(2), pp. 108–125.
11. Nuttbrock, Larry, Hwahng, Sel, Bockting, Walter, Rosenblum, Andrew, et al. (2010) "Psychiatric Impact of Gender-Related Abuse Across the Life Course of Male-to-Female Transgender Persons." *Journal of Sex Research*, 47(1), pp. 12–23.
12. Corliss, Heather L, Cochran, Susan D and Mays, Vickie M (2002) "Reports of parental maltreatment during childhood in a United States population-based survey of homosexual, bisexual, and heterosexual adults." *Child Abuse & Neglect*, 26(11), pp. 1165–1178.

13 Bandini, E, Fisher, A D, Ricca, V, Ristori, J, et al. (2011) "Childhood maltreatment in subjects with male-to-female gender identity disorder." *International Journal of Impotence Research*, 23(6), pp. 276–285.

14 Anon (1981) "Changes in patients with gender-identity problems after parental death." *American Journal of Psychiatry*, 138(1), pp. 41–45.

15 Lingiardi, Vittorio, Giovanardi, Guido, Fortunato, Alexandro, Nassisi, Valentina and Speranza, Anna Maria (2017) "Personality and Attachment in Transsexual Adults." *Archives of Sexual Behavior*, 46(5), pp. 1313–1323.

16 Cussino, Martina, Crespi, Chiara, Mineccia, Valentina, Molo, Mariateresa, et al. (2017) "Sociodemographic characteristics and traumatic experiences in an Italian transgender sample." *International Journal of Transgenderism*, 18(2), pp. 215–226.

17 Veale, Jaimie F., Clarke, Dave E. and Lomax, Terri C. (2008) "Sexuality of Male-to-Female Transsexuals." *Archives of Sexual Behavior*, 37(4), pp. 586–597.

18 Wharton, V. W. (2007) "Gender Variance and Mental Health: A National Survey of Transgender Trauma History, Posttraumatic Stress, and Disclosure in Therapy."

19 Wilchins, R. A. (2006) *"What does it cost to tell the truth?,"* in *The Transgender Studies Reader* Stryker, S. and Whittle, S. (eds.), New York City, Routledge.

20 Gehring, Darlynne and Knudson, Gail (2005) "Prevalence of Childhood Trauma in a Clinical Population of Transsexual People." *International Journal of Transgenderism*, 8(1), pp. 23–30.

21 Lothstein, L. M. (1983) *Female-to-Male Transsexualism: Historical, Clinical, and Theoretical Issues*, Abingdon, Routledge.

22 Pauly, Ira B. (1974) "Female transsexualism: Part I." *Archives of Sexual Behavior*, 3(6), pp. 487–507.

23 di Ceglie, D. (1998) *A Stranger in my Own Body: Atypical Gender Identity Development and Mental Health*, London, Karnac Books.

24 Devor, Holly (1994) "Transsexualism, Dissociation, and Child Abuse." *Journal of Psychology & Human Sexuality*, 6(3), pp. 49–72.

25 COATES, SUSAN and PERSON, ETHEL SPECTOR (1985) "Extreme Boyhood Femininity: Isolated Behavior or Pervasive Disorder?" *Journal of the American Academy of Child Psychiatry*, 24(6), pp. 702–709.

26 Hill, Darryl B. and Menvielle, Edgardo (2009) "'You Have to Give Them a Place Where They Feel Protected and Safe and Loved': The Views of Parents Who Have Gender-Variant Children and Adolescents." *Journal of LGBT Youth*, 6(2–3), pp. 243–271.

27 Zucker, K. J., and Bradley, S. J. (1995) *Gender Identity Disorder and Psychosexual Problems in Children and Adolescents.*, New York City, Guilford Press.

28 MARANTZ, SONIA, COATES, SUSAN, autonomy and practices, child-rearing (1991) "Mothers of Boys with Gender Identity Disorder: A Comparison of Matched Controls." *Journal of the American Academy of Child & Adolescent Psychiatry*, 30(2), pp. 310–315.

29 Zucker, Kenneth J. and Kuksis, Myra (1990) "Gender dysphoria and sexual abuse: A case report." *Child Abuse & Neglect*, 14(2), pp. 281–283.

30 Stoller, R. J. (1968) *Sex and Gender*, London, Karnac.

31 Money, J. (1986) *Lovemaps: Clinical Concepts of Sexual/Erotic Health and Pathology, Paraphilia, and Gender Transposition of Childhood, Adolescence, and Maturity*, London, Ardent Media.

32 Money, John and Lamacz, Margaret (1984) "Gynemimesis and gynemimetophilia: Individual and cross-cultural manifestations of a gender-coping strategy hitherto unnamed." *Comprehensive Psychiatry*, 25(4), pp. 392–403.

33 Macfie, Jenny, Cicchetti, Dante and Toth, Sheree L (2001) "Dissociation in maltreated versus nonmaltreated preschool-aged children." *Child Abuse & Neglect*, 25(9), pp. 1253–1267.

34 Fonagy, Peter, Target, Mary and Gergely, George (2000) "ATTACHMENT AND BORDERLINE PERSONALITY DISORDER." *Psychiatric Clinics of North America*, 23(1), pp. 103–122.

35 Cicchetti, D., and Valentino, K. (2006) *Developmental Psychopathology* 2nd ed. Cicchetti, D. and Cohen, D. J. (eds.), New York City.

36 Briere, John (2006) "Dissociative Symptoms and Trauma Exposure." *Journal of Nervous & Mental Disease*, 194(2), pp. 78–82.

37 Solomon, J. E., and George, C. E. (1999) *Attachment Disorganization*, New York City, Guilford Press.

38 Zilberstein, Karen (2014) "The use and limitations of attachment theory in child psychotherapy." *Psychotherapy*, 51(1), pp. 93–103.

39 Bailey, Heidi Neufeld, Moran, Greg and Pederson, David R. (2007) "Childhood maltreatment, complex trauma symptoms, and unresolved attachment in an at-risk sample of adolescent mothers." *Attachment & Human Development*, 9(2), pp. 139–161.

40 Courtois, C. A. (2004) "Complex trauma, complex reactions: assessment and treatment." *Psychotherapy*, pp. 412–425.

41 Steensma, Thomas D., Zucker, Kenneth J., Kreukels, Baudewijntje P. C., VanderLaan, Doug P., et al. (2014) "Behavioral and Emotional Problems on the Teacher's Report Form: A Cross-National, Cross-Clinic Comparative Analysis of Gender Dysphoric Children and Adolescents." *Journal of Abnormal Child Psychology*, 42(4), pp. 635–647.

42 Steensma, Thomas D., McGuire, Jenifer K., Kreukels, Baudewijntje P.C., Beekman, Anneke J. and Cohen-Kettenis, Peggy T. (2013) "Factors Associated With Desistence and Persistence of Childhood Gender Dysphoria: A Quantitative Follow-Up Study." *Journal of the American Academy of Child & Adolescent Psychiatry*, 52(6), pp. 582–590.

43 Steensma, Thomas D., Biemond, Roeline, de Boer, Fijgje and Cohen-Kettenis, Peggy T. (2011) "Desisting and persisting gender dysphoria after childhood: A qualitative follow-up study." *Clinical Child Psychology and Psychiatry*, 16(4), pp. 499–516.

44 Nguyen, Hillary B., Loughead, James, Lipner, Emily, Hantsoo, Liisa, et al. (2019) "What has sex got to do with it? The role of hormones in the transgender brain." *Neuropsychopharmacology*, 44(1), pp. 22–37.

45 Holmes, David (2016) "Brain imaging: Cross-sex hormones alter grey matter structures." *Nature Reviews Endocrinology*, 12(12), p. 686.

46 Reardon, Sara (2019) "The largest study involving transgender people is providing long-sought insights about their health." *Nature*, 568(7753), pp. 446–449.

47	Goldman, Bruce (2017) "How men's and women's brains are different	Stanford Medicine." *Stanford Medicine.* [online] Available from: https://stanmed.stanford.edu/2017spring/how-mens-and-womens-brains-are-different.html (Accessed 1 July 2022)
48	Alter, Charlotte (2022) "Transgender Men See Sexism From Both Sides." *Time.* [online] Available from: https://time.com/transgender-men-sexism/ (Accessed 1 July 2022)
49	Yong, Ed (2008) "Brains of gay people resemble those of straight people of opposite sex." *National Geographic.* [online] Available from: https://www.nationalgeographic.com/science/article/brains-of-gay-people-resemble-those-of-straight-people-of-opposite-sex (Accessed 1 July 2022)
50	Greene, Chad Felix (2021) "Activists Try To Ban Researchers From Studying Transgender People." *The Federalist.* [online] Available from: https://thefederalist.com/2021/02/15/leftist-activists-try-to-ban-researchers-from-studying-transgender-people/ (Accessed 1 July 2022)
51	Brewster, Lee G. (1977) "Post-Op Transsexual Commits Suicide - Operation Was a Mistake." *Drag* Vol 7, No 25. [online] Available from: https://archive.org/details/drag725unse/page/6/mode/2up (Accessed 23 June 2022)
52	Brewster, Lee G. (1977) "Ihlenfeld Explains Why He'll No Longer Treat Transsexuals." *Drag Vol. 6 No. 23*, p. 6.
53	Knox, Liam (2019) "Media's 'detransition' narrative is fueling misconceptions, trans advocates say." *NBC News.* [online] Available from: https://www.nbcnews.com/feature/nbc-out/media-s-detransition-narrative-fueling-misconceptions-trans-advocates-say-n1102686 (Accessed 1 July 2022)
54	Turban, Jack L., Loo, Stephanie S., Almazan, Anthony N. and Keuroghlian, Alex S. (2021) "Factors Leading to 'detransition' among Transgender and Gender Diverse People in the United States: A Mixed-Methods Analysis." *LGBT Health*, 8(4), pp. 273–280.
55	Murad, Mohammad Hassan, Elamin, Mohamed B., Garcia, Magaly Zumaeta, Mullan, Rebecca J., et al. (2010) "Hormonal therapy and sex reassignment: a systematic review and meta-analysis of quality of life and psychosocial outcomes." *Clinical Endocrinology*, 72(2), pp. 214–231.
56	Bess, J. and Stabb, Sally (2009) "The Experiences of Transgendered Persons in Psychotherapy: Voices and Recommendations." *Journal of Mental Health Counseling*, 31(3), pp. 264–282.
57	Ford, Zack (2016) "'Was just sent a music video with a trans affirming message but a cis man playing a trans woman. I told them I wouldn't be sharing it.' @ZackFord." *Twitter.* [online] Available from: https://twitter.com/ZackFord/status/792043312815476738?ref_src=twsrc%5Etfw%7Ctwcamp%5Etweetembed%7Ctwterm%5E792043312815476738%7Ctwgr%5Ehb_2_10%7Ctwcon%5Es1_&ref_url=https%3A%2F%2Fwww.huffpost.com%2Fentry%2Fif-transphobia-exists-it-is-entirely-the-lgbt-movements_b_5814b28be4b08301d33e0a25 (Accessed 2 July 2022)
58	Byrne, Mya (2016) "Dear Mark Ruffalo, Timothy McNeil And Matt Bomer: Why Is Matt Bomer Playing ATrans Woman?	HuffPost Communities." *Huffington Post.* [online] Available from: https://www.huffpost.com/entry/an-open-letter-from-a-

trans-woman-to-mark-ruffalo-timothy_b_57c72598e4b07addc4102dd4 (Accessed 2 July 2022)

59 Clayton, Jamie (2016) "'I really hope you both choose to do some actual good for the trans community one day.' @MsJamieClayton." *Twitter*.

60 Greene, Chad Felix (2016) "If 'Transphobia' Exists, it is Entirely The LGBT Movement's Doing | HuffPost Contributor." *Huffington Post*. [online] Available from: https://www.huffpost.com/entry/if-transphobia-exists-it-is-entirely-the-lgbt-movements_b_5814b28be4b08301d33e0a25 (Accessed 2 July 2022)

61 Mock, Janet (2014) "Janet Mock's Sex Work Experiences as a Young Trans Woman | Janet Mock." *JanetMock.com*. [online] Available from: https://janetmock.com/2014/01/30/janet-mock-sex-work-experiences/ (Accessed 2 July 2022)

62 Vagianos, Alanna (2017) "Janet Mock: Sex Workers' Rights Must Be Part Of The Women's March | HuffPost Communities." *Huffington Post*. [online] Available from: https://www.huffpost.com/entry/janet-mock-sex-workers-rights-must-be-part-of-the-womens-march_n_587f798ae4b01cdc64c8a16d (Accessed 2 July 2022)

63 Manning, Chelsea E. (2017) "Chelsea E. Manning on Twitter: '@CanIGetAWhitney because not getting medical attention for trans people is fatal' / Twitter." *Twitter*. [online] Available from: https://twitter.com/xychelsea/status/884188432955654144 (Accessed 2 July 2022)

64 Ford, Zack (2014) "Leelah Alcorn And The Quiet Genocide Of Transgender People – ThinkProgress." *ThinkProgress*. [online] Available from: https://archive.thinkprogress.org/leelah-alcorn-and-the-quiet-genocide-of-transgender-people-83eae6117949/ (Accessed 2 July 2022)

65 Dhejne, Cecilia, Lichtenstein, Paul, Boman, Marcus, Johansson, Anna L. v., et al. (2011) "Long-Term Follow-Up of Transsexual Persons Undergoing Sex Reassignment Surgery: Cohort Study in Sweden" Scott, J. (ed.). *PLoS ONE*, 6(2), p. e16885. [online] Available from: https://dx.plos.org/10.1371/journal.pone.0016885 (Accessed 2 July 2022)

66 Greene, Chad Felix (2017) "Transgender Suicides: What to Do About Them - Public Discourse." *Public Discourse*. [online] Available from: https://www.thepublicdiscourse.com/2017/07/19769/ (Accessed 2 July 2022)

67 CDC (n.d.) "Sexual Risk Behaviors Can Lead to HIV, STDs, & Teen Pregnancy | Adolescent and School Health | CDC." [online] Available from: https://www.cdc.gov/healthyyouth/sexualbehaviors/ (Accessed 2 July 2022)

68 CDC (n.d.) "Risk and Protective Factors|Sexual Violence|Violence Prevention|Injury Center|CDC." [online] Available from: https://www.cdc.gov/violenceprevention/sexualviolence/riskprotectivefactors.html (Accessed 2 July 2022)

69 Regnerus, Mark (2017) "No Long-Term Harm? The New Scientific Silence on Child-Adult Sex and the Age of Consent - Public Discourse." *Public Discourse*. [online] Available from: https://www.thepublicdiscourse.com/2017/09/20057/ (Accessed 2 July 2022)

70 Greene, Chad Felix (2017) "I Was an Eight-Year-Old Drag Queen - Public Discourse." *Public Discourse*. [online] Available from: https://www.thepublicdiscourse.com/2017/10/20124/ (Accessed 2 July 2022)

71   Hilton, Brandon (2018) "Brandon Hilton on Twitter: 'I think this new generation of drag kids is brilliant and inspiring! @Desmond_Amazing and Lactatia are the future! @TheHouseofMann is just making sure they look SICKENING! people will talk no matter what, might as well give them something FIERCE to look at! https://t.co/Vx5JB7aFvL' / Twitter." *Twitter*. [online] Available from: https://twitter.com/BRANDONHILTON/status/949731129472503808 (Accessed 2 July 2022)

72   Hilton, Brandon (2018) "Brandon Hilton on Twitter: 'woke up to countless tweets telling me "kill yourself" and calling me a "pedo" after we announced 9 year old drag superstar Lactatia as our new HOUSE OF MANN covergirl... If you can't handle a kid in a sequin onesie, maybe the future isn't for you! https://t.co/7HPbwzbMYX' / Twitter." *Twitter*. [online] Available from: https://twitter.com/BRANDONHILTON/status/949728983897296897 (Accessed 2 July 2022)

73   Broverman, Neal (2017) "Meet 8-Year-Old Drag Queen Lactatia." *Advocate*. [online] Available from: https://www.advocate.com/youth/2017/6/05/meet-8-year-old-drag-queen-lactatia (Accessed 2 July 2022)

74   Greene, Chad Felix (2018) "LGBT Activists Can't See What's Wrong With A 9-Year-Old Drag Queen." *The Federalist*. [online] Available from: https://thefederalist.com/2018/01/16/lgbt-activists-cant-see-whats-wrong-9-year-old-drag-queen/ (Accessed 2 July 2022)

75   Greene, Chad, Felix (2018) "Here's Why I Choose Life Instead Of Ending It Like My Dad Did." *The Federalist*. [online] Available from: https://thefederalist.com/2018/06/12/heres-choose-life-instead-ending-like-dad/ (Accessed 2 July 2022)

76   @4th_WaveNow (2018) "4thWaveNow on Twitter: 'Surprise. MTF trans activists are outraged that a reporter dared to listen to thoughtful parents and their teen daughters who formerly identified as trans but have now desisted. We will update this thread as more pile on. https://t.co/eiVCjNCj21' / Twitter." *Twitter*. [online] Available from: https://twitter.com/4th_WaveNow/status/1008737314242269184 (Accessed 2 July 2022)

77   Singal, Jesse (2018) "When Children Say They're Transgender - The Atlantic." *The Atlantic*. [online] Available from: https://www.theatlantic.com/magazine/archive/2018/07/when-a-child-says-shes-trans/561749/ (Accessed 2 July 2022)

78   Canter, James (2016) " Sexology Today!: Do trans- kids stay trans- when they grow up?" *Sexology Today!* [online] Available from: http://www.sexologytoday.org/2016/01/do-trans-kids-stay-trans-when-they-grow_99.html (Accessed 2 July 2022)

79   Greene, Chad Felix (2018) "Atlantic Article Should Foster Consensus That Trans Is For Adults Only." *The Federalist*. [online] Available from: https://thefederalist.com/2018/06/21/atlanticsarticle-foster-consensus-transgenderism-adults/ (Accessed 2 July 2022)

80   Greene, Chad, Felix (2018) "My Rape Doesn't Justify Punishing People Without Due Process." *The Federalist*. [online] Available from:

	https://thefederalist.com/2018/09/19/man-raped-doesnt-justify-punishing-people-without-due-process/ (Accessed 2 July 2022)
81	Greene, Chad Felix (2019) "Even Though I Feel Non-Binary, Identifying As My Sex Makes Sense." *The Federalist*. [online] Available from: https://thefederalist.com/2019/02/07/gender-redefining-activists-demands-are-silly-and-imposing/ (Accessed 2 July 2022)
82	Greene, Chad Felix (2021) "How Ryan Anderson's Banned Book Helped Me With Gender Dysphoria." *The Federalist*. [online] Available from: https://thefederalist.com/2021/03/01/how-ryan-andersons-banned-book-when-harry-became-sally-helped-me-with-gender-dysphoria/ (Accessed 2 July 2022)

Printed in Great Britain
by Amazon